A shrewd and hilarious guide to keeping your end up at the office and in married life

WORK AND WEDLOCK

Here in a single volume are two of Jilly Cooper's best-selling books: the complete texts of *How to Survive From Nine to Five* and *How to Stay Married*

D1376259

Jilly Cooper

WORK AND WEDLOCK

(combining in one volume the complete texts of
How to Survive from Nine to Five
and *How to Stay Married*)

drawings by
TIMOTHY JAQUES

MAGNUM BOOKS
Methuen Paperbacks Ltd

A Magnum Book

WORK AND WEDLOCK
ISBN 0 417 01820 7

This first combined paperback edition of
How to Survive from Nine to Five and *How to Stay Married*
first published 1977 by Methuen Paperbacks Ltd
11 New Fetter Lane, London EC4P 4EE
How to Survive from Nine to Five first published 1970
How to Stay Married first published 1969
by Methuen & Co Ltd

Text Copyright © 1969, 1970, 1977 by Jilly Cooper

Drawings © 1969 and 1970 by Methuen & Co Ltd

Magnum Books are published
by Methuen Paperbacks Ltd 11 New Fetter Lane,
London EC4P 4EE
Printed in Great Britain by Richard Clay
(The Chaucer Press) Ltd, Bungay, Suffolk

Contents

HOW TO SURVIVE FROM
NINE TO FIVE

HOW TO STAY MARRIED

How to survive
from nine to five

To Derek and Christine

introduction

From the conservative dark
Into the ethical life
The dense commuters come
Repeating their morning vow
I *will* be true to the wife,
I'll concentrate more on my work.

W. H. Auden.

It is nearly nine years since I had a proper nine to five job, but as I sit here typing in the garden looking at a torrent of bright pink roses, and watching my son dig up plants and sprinkle earth over the cats, I am still haunted by the days I spent working in an office.

Offices, you see, are for organization men, and I–being a dyed-in-the-wool disorganization woman–was a disaster as an employee, getting through more than twenty jobs in thirteen years.

My first job, which was the only one I really loved, was as a cub reporter on a local paper. The editor was a wild Irishman who wrote like a dream when he wasn't drinking like a fish. At the end of six months, he amazed the inhabitants of the town by walking the length of the High Street with a pink plastic chamber-pot on his head. A week later I came in on Monday morning to find him crouched on top of his desk, squawking morosely, an empty whiskey bottle beside him.

"I'm a seagull," he said after a few minutes, "and I shall fly around and do it on anybody I don't like."

At lunchtime, the Office Crone noticed him and immediately telephoned the newspaper proprietor at head office. Later in the day, a plain van came to take him away.

I'm a seagull

It was the first instance of many in office life when the right but repulsive prevailed over the wrong but romantic. After that a more sober editor was appointed, but the job never again reached the same peaks of inspired lunacy, and a few months later, lured by Mayfair and the fleshpots, I left journalism to become an account executive in a public relations firm.

After that the jobs came fast and furious – copywriter, editor, publisher's reader, receptionist for a motor firm, demonstrator at Earl's Court, temporary typist, a nymphomation officer in advertising, a telephonist, a puppy-fat model, and finally even a director of a company. So I can say truthfully that I have a non-working knowledge of most levels of the office caste system.

Offices, I found, were too much like school. There was the same nightmarish first day, when it was better to be seen and not heard, the same hierarchy, where it was not done to make close friends with one's seniors or one's juniors, the Personnel Department in a permanent state of bossy bustle like Matron and her minions, the notice boards on which pointless messages were pinned, lunches in the canteen exactly like school dinners, the responsible members of the staff behaving like form prefects, board meetings like staff meetings ('what are they saying, are they discussing me?') and finally, whether you're a writer or a typist, the awful sense of handing in your prep and having it returned the next day: 'C+. Could do better.'

The only difference is that as schools get paid (instead of paying you for your services) they are less trigger happy about booting you out than offices are.

I was the one that got away, but I still think of the thousands of people fighting their way to the office every morning.

Getting a job

Having had so many jobs in my life, I consider myself an expert at interviews. Never be depressed by the high-powered-sounding advertisements on the Appointments pages, the columns and columns of ads offering *unique* opportunities at attractive salaries to the right candidate: "We are looking for a young dynamic engineer," they say, "someone with drive and enthusiasm and a keen interest in re-inforced concrete, who is willing to settle in Australia. A knowledge of explosives would be useful."

The Advertising ones are even worse: "We at Fishbone, Codpiece and Nutter aren't afraid of competition. We're looking for a young creative genius who can write us all into the ground."

Hey there, Girl Friday

The sits. vac. for persons aren't much better: "Hey there, Eunuch Friday. I'm looking for someone to step into my shoes (size nine) and look after the most lovable Production Manager in the world. I wouldn't be deserting him if I weren't expecting a baby next month. Luncheon Vouchers, sickness

benefit" (morning presumably) "three weeks holiday."
They're always wanting: "Very fast shorthand typists"
when you have given up sex for Lent, or offering
"Mature persons periods of exposure at Board Level",
whatever that may mean.

Even when you've found the kind of job you're looking
for, there are phrases to watch: "The successful
candidate will be expected to deputise for the departmental head in his absence," which means the
departmental head is probably an alcoholic or a sex
maniac.

"We're looking for a person who can introduce staff
changes where necessary." They're chicken about
doing their own sacking.

"Capable, unflappable person, who is not afraid of
hard work needed for busy office." They're a lot of
layabouts, and you'll be flat out from 9 a.m. to 9 p.m.

The letter of application is the next hurdle. It should
be a masterpiece of fiction, papering over all the cracks.
Get it properly typed on decent writing paper. Never
let it run over the page, people get bored with reading.
Never send a roncoed curriculum vitae, or start off:
"Dear Sir, You need me/I'm the man you are looking
for," which automatically puts people off.

If you've changed jobs many times, pick out the five
most impressive ones, and pretend they lasted longer
than they did. Always conceal long patches when you
were out of work. Never say you left a job for "personal
reasons". No one will believe you.

Before you're given an interview you may well be sent
one of those terrible questionnaires to fill in about
what games you excelled in at school, and whether the
parrot's had any serious illness and what sex you are.
Pure 1984. Resist the temptation to mob them up. Be
careful, too, of those eleven plus psychology tests:
"Which is the odd man out—goat, ardvaak, warthog,
giraffe, snuffbox, goose, Tramps?" It's sure not to be

Tramps.

If they ask you to pick out the doodle you like best avoid the one with lots of squiggles, which means you're over-sexed, and avoid circles outside the triangle, which is supposed to prove that you're too homeloving and will rush out of the office at four thirty every afternoon.

WHAT TO WEAR AT THE INTERVIEW MEN

The most expensive cigars

For the budding executive you still can't go wrong with tapered charcoal and the old school tie. But at present, there is a swing away from the pink-and-white-faced Etonian with his rolled umbrella, so you may do better to wear a corduroy suit, no tie and flatten your 'a's when you talk. Exude an air of affluence, rich but not gaudy, silk shirt, gold cuff links, aftershave. Never smoke, especially if you've got bitten nails, but if you must, let it be the most expensive cigars (never from the packet or the tin). This is particularly imposing in a woman.

If you're applying for any kind of creative post, however – designer, copywriter etc. – the wilder you look the better: beards, jerseys inside your shirt, medallions, everything hanging round your neck except women. Get a calligrapher to write your letter of application for you, and remember to say nothing at the interview—as they expect young genius to be totally inarticulate.

Be careful about too long or too short hair. Equal pay for women is the law now—but the prejudices remain.

GIRLS

I suppose I never dressed so well in any office where I worked as on the first time I crossed the threshold. I became such an expert at bulling myself up for the interview, they never recognised me when I turned up in my normal scruff order on the first day of work.

Always tie your hair back. I once learnt that I was turned down for one job purely because mine fell over my eyes. The choice of scent is tricky. Plump optimistically for *Je Reviens* if you are seeing a man, *4711* if it's a woman. And it's a good idea to carry a spotless pair of gloves in a paper bag, to be whisked out just before you go into the interview.

Make-up is a more difficult problem. Will the bedroom eyes conceal the bedpost legs? And if you tart up too much there are always those direct males who are far more interested in offering you extra-mural activities: "I haven't anything for you right now, Miss Nitwit-Thompson, but let me take down your particulars. 722-4910 did you say? Splendid, splendid."

I haven't anything for you, Miss Nitwit-Thompson

THE INTERVIEW PROPER

Go to lots of interviews, at least one a month even when you don't need a job, to keep in training for when you do.

There are several important points to bear in mind.

1. Never reveal you're out of work even if your wife, children and parrot are starving. Jobs are like sex, the harder you play to get, the more they want you. Give the impression you can take or leave their lousy job.

2. Look cheerful. A chum of mine who deserves a degree in amiability went after a very high-powered advertising job. The interview had only lasted two minutes when the telephone went, it was the interviewer's mistress on the line and he discussed a forthcoming jaunt to Paris with her for the next twenty-five minutes, by which time the next candidate was due. My chum had just sat there looking amiable and unembarrassed. To his amazement he got the job, and later when he looked up details of his interview in the Confidential File, it said: "Keen,

co-operative, a good mixer, asked deeply searching questions about the nature of our business."

Boast about your capabilities

3. Remember to boast about your capabilities. Any idiot can sit on a board or take a job at chief executive level. But be careful of claiming specialised knowledge like space selling, or you may find yourself orbiting the earth and not able to get down.

4. If you're interviewed by the managing director, Mr Compton Ricket, and on the wall hangs a portrait of the late Sir Angus Compton Ricket, and suddenly

young Mr Compton Ricket, just down from Oxford, pops in so Daddy can OK his expenses, don't touch the job. You'll find there are seven deadly sons between you and that seat on the Board.

5. Phrases like "Only £15,000, the fringe benefits had better be good", never go amiss.

6. Too many people, when they go for interviews, are more interested in giving a good impression than finding out what the job is about. Remember it's you who ask the questions:

You: Why did the previous chap leave?

Interviewer: Of his own accord.

You: Not satisfied with working for you, eh?

7. Always put the interviewer at his ease. As soon as you enter the room, tell him to sit down and smoke if he likes.

8. An excellent precaution is to ask the interviewer to give you references from three previous employees.

9. Never sign a contract before you've sorted out paid holidays, free houses, free cars, bonus, pension, etc. You won't be in a position to bargain once they've got you in their clutches.

10. Finally, there's the question of references. You must have some mates willing to perjure themselves and add a few handles to their names.

Your euphoria at landing a plum job will soon give way to dismay, then panic, as your month's notice comes to an end. Will anyone speak to you; have you oversold yourself; will you be able to hold down the job?

You will suddenly become very loth to leave your old colleagues, particularly when they give you a riotous send off and club together to buy you a gilt tray or one piece of everything belonging to a dinner service you've always wanted. Don't forget to thank them. The letter will be pinned on the notice board and should begin:

'Dear All,

Denise and I were delighted with the tea tray you so kindly gave me. We have put it on the mantelpiece in the lounge, and it will serve as a constant and happy reminder of all the good times I had at No. 48.'

The newcomer

THE FIRST DAY

The first day at any office is absolute hell. When I'm king I shall make it law that everyone starts a new job on Friday instead of Monday. Monday morning, in particular, couldn't be a worse time. All the incumbents are feeling anti-establishment, ill tempered and are desperately trying to catch up on all those very urgent things that didn't seem to matter a damn on Friday.

Monday morning is also No Man's Land, a limbo between home and the office. The staff have been isolated from each other for two days over the weekend, and have lost any corporate enthusiasm, which will only emerge about Thursday. By Friday it will be joined by excitement about the coming weekend and they will feel in a good enough mood to give newcomers the welcome they deserve.

As it is, you arrive about 8.30 sick with nerves to find the building locked or deserted except for the odd cleaner morosely pushing a squeegee over the floor. You then kick your heels in Reception until a few 'sekketries' (as they describe themselves) arrive from the country lugging pigskin suitcases and the pick of Daddy's herbaceous border (which will either be arranged in jam jars, or block the basins of the Ladies for the rest of the week).

About eleven o'clock, Miss Hitler from Personnel will bustle up and cause a rumpus because you've forgotten your P.45 and your insurance cards. She will then direct you to your office. If you are an executive you will either find an in-tray groaning with bucks other people have passed, or even worse, a completely bare desk with empty drawers and an empty filing cabinet, and you'll sit gazing at a huge sheet of virgin blotting paper, wondering what to write with all those sharpened pencils.

It's also possible that there's no job and you've just been brought in to swell the shadow Managing Director's faction in office politics. The sekketry promised you has decided to work for someone else (a blessing because you've no work for her anyway) and the rest of the department are wearing black ties and flying the Office Crone at half mast in mourning for your predecessor, whom they consider was unfairly ousted.

Occasionally people will shuffle into your office and say: "Oh, you're the new chap," and shuffle out again. Endeavour to appear busy. One man I know brought in at a very senior level wrote a novel during his first three months. Thinking he was writing reports, everyone was deeply impressed. Ask for progress reports for the last year (this will throw them, because they probably don't have any), or files, or the minutes of recent meetings. Then you can fill in your time, shuffling papers back and forth, frowning and nodding gravely. Soft pedal the hatchet approach: "I'm a new chap, just getting my sea legs, perhaps you can help me," will work wonders.

If you join as a sekketry you will probably be fobbed off with a desk with uneven legs, and an old battleship of a typewriter which everyone else has rejected and which tabulates automatically every time you press the A key.

An old battleship of a typewriter

Suddenly a choleric, fire-breathing old man will rush out of a nearby office, shout at you and rush back again. Alas, that is the cosy pink-faced sherry-bestowing old gentleman who seemed such a darling when he interviewed you last month. Bosses are invariably April when they woo, December when they wed. He wants you to take dictation.

Nearby sekketries will not speak to you except to tell you what a snake he is, and that everyone's leaving the firm because he's so vile to work for. You daren't interrupt their Monday morning panic with questions, so you will automatically have to re-type all your letters tomorrow because you didn't know about the lilac flimsy for the Art Department, or not putting a full stop after the date.

Remember to bring in two large shopping baskets to smuggle out all the botched-up letters you have to throw away. Miss Hitler from Personnel will not be amused by those brimming waste-paper baskets of scrumpled paper.

You will sit crossing your legs wondering how much longer you can hold out because no one has told you the firm shares a loo with Golberg's Imported Goatskins on the next floor.

At twelve-fifteen someone looks at her watch and says with obvious relief, "I should go to lunch now", then they can all discuss you.

Not knowing where to go, you will be deceived by the peeling paint and gloomy exterior of a little place on the corner which will turn out to be French and cost you at least a fiver.

Then there's the ghastly prospect when you get back to the office dead on 1.15 of how you're going to survive until 5. Although the work is piling up, you're terrified to type because you do it so slowly compared with the rest of the sekketries, whose hands are moving over the keys with the speed and dexterity of concert pianists. By tea time you're so grateful to some whiskery old boot for offering you a Lincoln cream that you strike up a friendship you'll never be able to shake off.

There are, however, advantages in being a newcomer. Everyone expects you to be inoperative for the first six months anyway, and you can blame every mistake you make on your predecessor.

On my father's first day at Fords, he was sent down to the foundry to report to the chief metallurgist. When he arrived one man seemed to be giving all the orders, so he turned to a nearby workman and asked if this man was the metallurgist.

"No Buddy," came the reply, "I think he's a Russian."

The hierarchy

Give people enough rope, and they'll hang you.

If you are to survive from nine to five, you must understand that nothing is more rigid than the office caste system, which is based on the premise that subordinates, unless kept ruthlessly in their place, will cheek you when you try to pull rank on them.

It is therefore unwise to risk being seen more than once in the company of a high-ranking member of the firm; people will suspect sexual commitment or political intrigue.

Nor is it done for women executives to go to lunch with the sekketries unless it's a birthday treat. Also, remember that if one of your old mates is promoted over you, your relationship will never be the same again. In no time he'll be goose-stepping all over you – power élite swagger and all.

Members of the staff, however, are always trying to wriggle their way up the hierarchy, typists calling themselves sekketries, sekketries calling themselves personal assistants, senior sekketries signing themselves Sekketry to the Deputy Managing Director whenever the Managing Director goes on holiday.

There will also be ridiculous wrangling over whether you are high enough up the ladder to rate a teaspoon or a bone china tea set with roses on it. In some firms they even have a special directors' lavatory, the only difference being that they have two kinds of loo paper – hard and very hard. If a woman were promoted to the board, it would be interesting to see if she would be expected to use it.

Your actual hierarchy will most probably consist of:
The Office Junior who knows nothing and does everything.
The Sekketry who knows everything and does nothing.

The Office Deb who knows everybody, my dear, and does nothing.

The pink and white Etonian trainee who knows the Office Deb.

The Personal Assistant who knows nothing and does nothing.

The Executive who interferes and prevents everyone from doing anything.

The Deputy Head of Department who panics.

The Head of the Department who signs letters, writes his report and doesn't give a damn because he's retiring at the end of the year.

The Managing Director, who can't read anyway.

Let us now look more closely at a few members of the hierarchy.

THE BOSS

Work hard and you will be rewarded by the promotion of your superiors.

Some bosses are good, some are not. Try very hard to give yours some responsibility. Bosses with nothing to do will always poke their noses into your affairs.

Here are some typical bosses:

THE BULLY

He can't leave his staff alone and bullies them into a state of jibbering inefficiency because it makes him feel superior. Stress is transmitted down the hierarchy until even the messenger boys are on tranquilizers. Like the circumlocution office, the bully is always beforehand in the art of seeing how not to do things. Stand up to him, or leave immediately before mental paralysis sets in.

THE MAN ON THE MAKE

He certainly won't want to make you, you're not important enough. He'll be far too busy sucking up to senior sekketries and the Managing Director's wife.

He will take credit if anything goes right, but you will carry the can if anything goes wrong.

A favourite expression will be: "I'm going to give you a free hand with this one," (but he'll keep a free foot to boot you out if you make a hash of it.) Or "You're going to have rather fun with this," before he hands you 20 pages of figures to type.

THE DREAMING BOFFIN

You'll spend your time sewing on buttons, collecting brief cases from the lost property office and rushing in with the fire extinguisher when he sets his waste-paper basket on fire. When he dictates he will probably eat his biscuits, then your biscuit, then drink his tea, then your tea. He will carry his washing round in his brief case, and suddenly pull out his underpants by mistake and say: "Would you possibly mind typing this for me?"

THE ARISTOCRAT

Work for him and you've got a cushy number. He will wear tweeds on Thursday for going to the country and he will not return until Tuesday morning. He will also be inoperative during the summer months, going to Ascot and Henley etc. Your time will be spent answering invitations, ordering caviar from Fortnums, and finding out how to address Duchesses and Earls on envelopes.

Moving down the hierarchy we come to:

THE EXECUTIVE

Avoid thought, it inevitably clouds the issue.

The executive has nothing to do except decide what is to be done, tell someone to do it, listen to reasons why they shouldn't do it, or why it should be done differently, and think up a crushing and conclusive reply. A week later he will follow up to see the thing has been done, discover it has not been done, ask why it hasn't been done, and listen to excuses from the person who didn't do it.

He will then wait another week before making further investigations, and avoid the temptation to wonder why he didn't do it himself in the first place. It would have taken him five minutes, instead it has taken a fortnight to find out that someone has taken at least a week to do it wrong. He then sits back and decides it's good for subordinates to learn by their own mistakes.

DEADWOOD

Nothing venture, nothing lose.

A step further down the hierarchy you will find the men the bosses hang their coats on – poor old dodderers in their late fifties, their false teeth rattling with nerves. Loss of pension hangs over their heads like a sword of Damocles. Knowing that they won't get another job if they're fired, they refuse to stick their necks out.

Weighed down by megaworries, the Dodderer will be convinced that people who couldn't even plot their way to the loo are conspiring against him. Shut doors will drive him into a frenzy, and every time he hears a typist whispering, even if it's only asking her next door neighbour if she can borrow a tampax, he's convinced she's whispering about him.

Home-made fishpaste sandwiches

At lunchtime, he takes a packet of home-made fishpaste sandwiches out of a shabby brief case. Occasionally at weekends, he gets drunk on Guinness. He often develops crushes on ugly typists.

Beneath this trembling exterior, however, lies a knight of the festering grievance, who can generate quite a force of discontent around the office.

Avoid antagonising him. He sneaks like wildfire.

PIGGIES

Piggies exist in most firms. They are sly, insensitive, unimaginative and always eating, particularly toffees, which they suck noisily and never offer to anyone else. Piggies never rise to the top of the tree, but they never get ulcers. They irritate subordinates and superiors equally, but are never fired because they are moderately efficient. Never work for a Piggy. Once you are directly below one in the hierarchy you will never rise to the top of the tree either.

THE PERSONNEL DEPARTMENT

Usually manned by a mini-bitch, who goes round measuring skirt lengths and calling sekketries by their surnames. Often she'll crouch for hours in the loo waiting to catch staff in indiscreet gossip.

Personnel are supposed to help you to hire people, but most of their day is spent forcing the squarest pegs into round holes. Whenever a new sekketry is required, they produce two identically grey, ugly, characterless girls to choose from.

Personnel departments are always having pointless economy drives. Even executives have to waste a ridiculous amount of time cajoling another biro out of them. In one office I remember the Personnel director hanging two rolls of lavatory paper, Bronco and Andrex, out of a top storey window to see which was the longer.

In another, the four members of the Personnel

department decided to go to Ireland together for the weekend on a special outing but insisted on flying on separate planes like the Royal Family, as the loss to the firm would have been so immeasurable if they had all been killed off in one go.

The Office Crone

THE OFFICE CRONE

She usually runs the typing pool. As soon as she arrives she puts on her mauve office cardigan to stop her 'good' clothes getting dirty. All her energies are channelled into bullying the typing pool like galley-slaves, and satisfying her insatiable appetite for new office equipment: dictaphones, electric typewriters, roller towels and Imperial Leather in the Ladies.

Much of her day will be spent foraging inside her transparent cream-coloured blouse to haul up a bra strap, eating biscuits, and surreptitiously plucking out her beard with a bulldog clip. She will be driven to frenzy by two things: lateness even if it's only thirty seconds, and mislaying her fingerette, which is a rubber thimble covered in spikes which looks like some weird Indian erotic device, but is actually used for turning pages quickly.

Sucking up is the only way to woo her. Hold her wool for her, ask her advice on beauty problems, give her the odd bar of Turkish Delight as a present.

One of her arch enemies will be:

Miss Nitwit-Thompson

THE OFFICE DEB

Miss Nitwit-Thompson, a decorative quarter-wit who comes wrapped in cashmere and scotch mist on the end of a long yellow Labrador. She is working for a pittance "because the job sounded so interesting," and is always having time off to go to mid-week weddings. She takes long weekends, and invariably rings Mummy on Friday and asks her to "stop the train".

Originally employed for her style and "lovely speaking voice" which would impress clients and Americans on the telephone. She is usually hogging the telephone making personal calls to Jeremy, Caroline or Fiona to discuss last night's ball.

Another of the Office Crone's sworn enemies is:

THE LITTLE HOME-BREAKER

The office sex kitten, who has a lived-in look about her and is far more preoccupied with outgoing males than outgoing mail. The only filing she does is to file her nails, and the only use she makes of the office pencil sharpener is to sharpen her eye-pencil and her claws. She is not to be dismissed, however, for she usually knows a lot of high-level secrets, leaked by chief executives in moments of passion. She is also quite capable of hooking the Managing Director, and suddenly becoming the Boss's wife.

THE LITTLE HOME-MAKER

Who puts sticky buds in jam jars on her boss's desk, and is always whisking round with a feather duster and percolating coffee. She will spend more time indulging her "office beautiful" pretensions than actually typing. When asked what she does at parties she will call herself a Personal Assistant.

THE UNDIPLOMATIC BAG

The senior sekketry who will guard her boss with such ferocity that she's quite likely to keep important clients and the Managing Director away from him until everyone forgets his existence. She will, however, be an excellent chucker-out if undesirables manage to insinuate themselves into his office.

Finally, we come to:

THE TYPING POOL

Generally called Maureen or Eileen. Their function in life seems to be to slop tea and type back letters that don't always make sense. If any of their carbons reach the files they will be spotted with rubbing-out smudges like a Dalmatian. Brainwashed by the system, they generally go to the loo in triplicate.

The Average Typist's Day, however, will go something like this:

9.10 Arrives generating bustle, hidden behind huge tinted spectacles, and muttering about de-railed carriages on the line. Disappears to the loo to tart up.

9.30 Removes typewriter cover, discusses what 'he' did and said last night, what television they saw, speculates on boss's mood, reads own and other typists' horoscopes in the morning papers.

10.00 Coffee break. Eats cheese roll.

10.15 Takes spare pair of shoes out of plastic bag in bottom drawer of desk. Changes into them.

10.30 Takes dictation.

10.45 Returns from dictation. Grumbles for thirty minutes about the horrible mood the boss is in.

11.15 Called to window by fellow typist to ogle comely man who is walking down the street. Snags tights on central heating, fills in hole with brown pencil.

11.40 Goes to loo to tart up.

12.00 Gone to dinner.

1.15 Returns with carrier bags, discusses dinner, eats Yoghurt and Mars Bar.

2.30 Boss comes back from lunch in better mood.

2.31 Goes to the loo to re-do face.

2.45 Tries to read shorthand back, holds book upside down.

3.00 Starts grumbling about non-arrival of tea.

3.15 Tea arrives, eats home-made cake out of paper bag, reads own and other typists' horoscopes in evening paper.

3.20 Types lethargically.

3.30 Slips out, ostensibly to the chemist's, so no one can ask why she's going.

4.00 Returns ostentatiously waving a Boots paper bag, which is actually full of make-up and tights.

4.10 Starts muttering about catching post, tidies ferociously for five minutes. Assembles one letter in large leather folder and gets it signed by boss.

4.30 Grabs floral plastic bag and joins queue for the loo for a good wash to get 'all the ink off my hands'.

4.45 Tears out of the office, muttering "must try and catch the early train tonight".

4.50 Building deserted.

THE OFFICE BOY

Office boys – the avant garde of the company – live in the postroom. In my day, they all used to smoke pot, strum guitars, and grow their hair halfway down their backs. Now they're all punk rockers. Invariably they get into trouble because the photographic machine decides to break down when they are photostating some writhing nude, or the roneo machine gives up the ghost when they are running off 500 copies of an obscene poem.

As an office boy you'll be paid a rotten salary, but you can make a bit on the side, taking buses whenever you have to deliver anything and charging up for a taxi.

The office boy's prime function is to give his superiors racing tips, keep them posted on what's top of the hit parade, and to rise eventually to Managing Director, so people can say: "I remember him when he was only an office boy."

When you get to the top, remember to sack all the

The office boy

people who knew you as an office boy. They won't take you seriously, and will instil lack of respect into their colleagues.

One office boy I know left a firm, made his packet and came back ten years later as a client. Not realising he had left, the Managing Director met him in the passage, handed him a parcel, and asked him to take it to the post office.

THE GRIPEVINE

"Our recording machine is broken—this is a person speaking."

Always chat up the switchboard girls, they wield

People who knew you as an office boy

enormous power. If you get across them they can 'forget' to take messages, keep you hanging about for hours waiting for a line, cut you off, and, worst of all, tip off Miss Hitler from Personnel that you've been making too many private calls—one of the most heinous of office crimes. They are also the hub of the gripevine and extremely valuable as a source of gossip. I also think that every member of the staff—particularly the men—should spend a day on the switchboard to see what pressures the telephonists are subjected to. I arrived at a temporary job once, and was asked if I could man the switchboard. No switchboard was ever more rapidly unmanned: all those horrible flaps signifying incoming calls came down at the same time, and the discs indicating that someone wanted a line started flickering as well. Flap, flap, flicker, flicker, they went all morning, until I was reduced to a state of nervous collapse. "Just putting you through," I would say hopefully, cutting off the sales manager's deal-clinching call to Australia for the seventh time.

On the receiving end there are those terrible occasions when the switchboard closes down and your lover, who's been soaking in some drinking club all afternoon, suddenly decides to ring you up and gets straight through to the Managing Director, who has to walk down three flights of stairs to find you.

Or those awful personal calls that come through when a meeting is being held in your office, and you hold the telephone very close to your ear so no one else in the room can hear the flood of invective.

Every so often there is a purge on private calls which no one takes any notice of. In one office a circle of paper was stuck on every telephone saying: "Please be brief. No private calls allowed." Some iconoclast promptly whipped it off and stuck it on the door of the Gents.

Survival for the top brass

HINTS FOR BOSSES

Let us begin with a few tips for the Boss – particularly if he's the Managing Director.

The secret of success is to keep your staff at each others' throats then they won't gang up against you. Create a state of tension and frantic backbiting. Divide and Rule.

Secure allegiance from junior executives by promising them individually that someone must step into your shoes when you retire. When you go away—on holiday or on a business trip—ask each one to keep an eye on things for you.

Don't humiliate the pants off a member of your staff in front of one of his subordinates.

Make decisions and stick to them. Havering is the one thing that will make you unpopular.

Try and remember your staff's names and use them when you meet them in the passage. Then if you want to put any of them down, call them by somebody else's name.

Be available at least sometime during the day to listen to grievances even if you do nothing about them.

Don't say you want to wish all your staff a Merry Christmas at 5 o'clock on Christmas Eve, and then ring down at 5.15 and say you're too busy.

Bosses could also do with a bit of advice in the way they handle their sekketries.

Ask about her lover or cats

You will reap dividends if you take a polite interest in her life outside the office. Ask her about her lover or her cats occasionally.

Remember her birthday. It's quite easy to check the date with Personnel and put it in your diary.

When she comes back from lunch three hours late, scarlet in the face, lacquered down to the eyebrows, and looking like a cross between Medusa and Little Lord Fauntleroy, tell her her hair looks nice.

One of the most damaging things people can say about you is: "He can't keep a sekketry." It's even worse than having V.D. Try not to turnover them too quickly.

HOW TO IMPRESS AS AN EXECUTIVE

Always give the impression you're working hard. It's like the story of the Messiah suddenly arriving at the Vatican. All the Vatican staff were thrown into a panic because they didn't know how to behave.

"It doesn't matter what you do," said the Pope. "Just look busy."

Or take a tip from the House of Lords throughout the war, who did nothing in particular but did it very well. Nothing gives a worse impression than an idle sekketry reading a book or painting her nails. Keep yours at full tilt, even if she's only typing her own personal letters with a pink and blue carbon underneath. If someone asks you if you're up to your ears, always say "yes". But if, on the other hand, your Managing Director wants you to do something worthwhile like Letrasetting a poster for his wife's baby show, agree to do it at once.

Suck up to the senior sekketries, admire their spangled hairnets, and drop Murray Mints into their pockets. This means they will sing your praises to their respective bosses, the directors, who probably don't gossip to anyone else. It will also ensure that you can get in to see the directors whenever you want to. Always chat up the directors' wives. The way to a man's heart is through his wife.

If you are over 26, get yourself married. Bachelors and queers are still, alas, regarded with suspicion. More often the former is assumed to be the latter.

Call your wife and children outlandish names like Brunhilda and Ethelred so the boss can remember them easily, and feel he's being good with you.

Whenever you get in early—get seen. Wander up and down the directors' floor with a piece of paper in your hand. Leave notes on people's desks: "*8.45*. Called in to see you; could you ring me back?" People never put the time on memos unless it's before or after hours.

Buy two identical overcoats which people identify as yours. Leave one hung up in your room when you leave the office early.

Only put in an appearance on Saturday morning when you know the Boss is going to be there.

Cultivate a good telephone manner:

"Bless you, bless you, lovely to talk to you, J.J., of course it's no trouble, we must meet and have lunch sometime, I'll ring you, bless you, love to Elizabeth, absolutely no trouble at all, bless you, bless you, well if you could pull the odd strings I'd be very grateful, all the best, J.J., goodbye." When you put down the receiver say, "Silly old bugger".

Get a night line plugged through to your office so that whenever a director wants one he's told you've already appropriated it and assumes you always work late.

Make yourself indispensable in some way. Be the only person who understands the crossest index system, or who has the energy to work out the table seating plan at the office dance.

Always be nice to everyone in the firm on the way up. You never know who you may meet on the way down. Most key managerial decisions are taken when the heads are down in the bunker. If the Managing Director is a golfer, take up golf, play it competently but don't beat him too often.

Games and sex are the only really reliable ways to bridge the hierarchy gap.

But don't beat him too often

Advice for the imperfect sekketry

Grumble first, think afterwards.

If your shorthand is slow, sit in front of your boss's desk in your shortest skirt and, whenever he starts dictating too fast, uncross and re-cross your legs very slowly. He'll stop in his tracks. Choose a boss whose office doesn't have Venetian blinds, then you can distract his attention by pointing out the Concorde or the first swallow when you need a moment to catch up. The tight sweater or the low-cut dress are the shoddy typist's allies. Hand him his letters, then stand with your hands behind your back or lean forward, and he won't notice any of the mistakes.

If you're going to be caught doing the crossword at least let it be *The Times*.

If you've got something terrible to confess, tell your boss in the afternoon when he comes back jolly from lunch, his mind scrambled with drink. Don't wait until five o'clock – when he will be suffering from a hangover. Remember, in office life godliness comes a very poor second to cleanliness. Tidy hair, white blouses, skirts on the knee making no concession to Maxi or Mini, polished shoes are the things which gladden the heart of the Office Crone and Miss Hitler from Personnel. If you get across them – no matter how much your boss loves you – you'll soon be out on your ear.

Today most offices allow you to wear trousers. But they must pass the Nice Trouser Test – you won't get away with split jeans or Bermuda shorts. Keep a communal skirt in the cupboard which any sekketry can borrow if she's summoned to one of the more reactionary directors.

Keep your office tidy. Nothing irks the powers-that-aren't more than an untidy office. They suspect, quite rightly, that all sorts of documents are hidden beneath the rubble. One of the reasons I was such a disaster in the office was that I always built ramparts of paper round me, in the hope that people might forget about me altogether.

Don't, on the other hand, go to the opposite extreme. Most bosses regard an empty desk as an indication

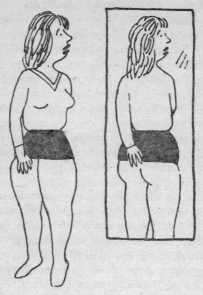

Keep a communal skirt

that you are under-employed. A few papers and files lying about will correct this impression.

Keep your out-tray from hitting the ceiling. One girl was sacked at one place I worked because, when told to do her boss's filing, she got languidly to her feet in front of the Personnel Dragon, picked up her boss's out-tray and calmly emptied it into the waste-paper basket.

Never, never throw any papers away – they're bound to be the one thing your boss asks you to turn up the very next day, so you spend fruitless hours scrabbling through dustbins full of empty tomato soup cans and cigarette butts.

THE PROTECTION RACKET

One of the sekketry's first duties is to cover up.

If the Managing Director wants your boss, even if he hasn't come in at all or left the building seven hours ago to "buy a packet of cigarettes," always say: "He's just popped out," or "He's in the building somewhere. I'll try and trace him."

After three o'clock never say he's not back from lunch, even if he isn't. It will give the impression he's lying on his back sozzled in El Vino's. Just say: "He popped in, and has just popped out again", or produce a tear-jerker excuse: "He's just slipped out to the shops to buy his wife/little daughter a birthday present."

THE TELEPHONE

Whatever your accent, as a sekketry you must put on a posh voice when you answer the telephone. If it's someone's sekketry wanting your boss, you will then have a tussle with her which may go on for hours over whose boss comes to the telephone first.

There are bound to be some people your boss will not want to talk to. If you're not sure say: "He's in a very important conference, I'll just see if he can be disturbed." Then find out if he will speak to them.

Or you can say: "He's tied up with the Managing Director's wife" (although it does give rise to terrifying bondage fantasies).

If you're stumped by a query, never betray ignorance, just say: "Oooo, my other telephone's ringing. I'll call you back later."

There are also ways of not revealing to your boss that you're making a personal call. Don't give a guilty start when he comes into the room and say nervously, "I must go now," and slam down the receiver.

Go on talking. Make remarks like: "That's extremely valuable, we must keep in close contact over this one. I'll find out some more details and figures and call you back later."

Then you can ring off and tell your boss it was a member of the public ringing up with some query, or a customer trying to flog you some office writing paper.

The office beautiful

Most people today are far too busy furnishing their offices to do any work. Half their day is spent firing off memos to the Personnel Department grumbling that the pile of their carpet is not deep enough and is a foot further away from the wall than the carpet of the man next door who has not been with the firm as long and is six months younger.

One of the reasons why bosses allow their staff to squander such vast amounts of the firm's money playing David Hicks is that if you make your office look like a "lovely home" they assume you're more likely to spend more time in it.

It's a mistake for the Managing Director to make his offices too lush. All the clients will think he's wasting their money, and all the staff will ask for rises.

But if he really wants to play the big tycoon he will paper his walls with grey flannel and cover the floor with a white shaggy rug. In one corner is a cocktail cabinet, in another a fridge for cooling down over-heated Office Crones. Six telephones sit on a huge black leather desk, along with the jade ashtrays, cigarette lighter and cigarette box filled with Russian cigarettes. No papers are in sight – it would be considered vulgar for anything like work to be carried on in such a rarefied atmosphere. Colleagues lounge on sofas round the room. Spotlights nestle in the walls casting pools of light on abstract paintings; after lunch they are dimmed so the maestro can cogitate or doze

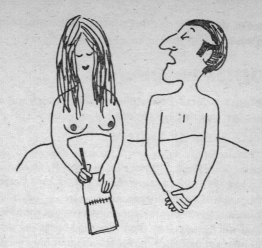

Like a "lovely home"

or finger his very private secretary in a reflective manner.

The smaller fry must be careful not to be too extreme. One copywriter I know moved into a top level post in an advertising agency and was determined that his office should be unique—no black leather, or reproduction tat breathing beeswax. He spent a fortune of the firm's money on William Morris wallpaper, an antique desk and chairs, a Victorian grandfather clock, and finally a harpsichord on which he strummed in moments of inspiration.

The trade papers got very excited and photographed him *in situ*, until the rest of the staff got so jealous they staged a palace revolution and had him removed. Later he was sent a bill for the office.

Piggies live in offices like sties, the top drawer of their desks filled with toffee papers and cake crumbs. They are also sly enough to put a photograph of the Prime Minister or the Leader of the Opposition on their walls, depending on the political affiliations of the Managing Director.

Office happenings

There are certain occupations in offices which will not only get you through the day but also impress people.

THE MEMORANDUM

"The horror of that moment," the King went on, *"I shall never, never forget!" "You will, though,"* the Queen said, *"if you don't make a memorandum of it."* Lewis Carroll.

Although it is the biggest time-waster in office life, you must never underrate the importance of the memo. You will be judged by the volume of your paper work. In offices today, the internal telephone is only used to conduct an affaire. If you ring a colleague up and tell him something important about work, he will wait patiently until you've finished, not listening to a word, and then say: "But you'll be sending me a memo about it anyway, won't you?"

The memo's chief function, however, is as a track-coverer, so that you can turn on someone six months later and snarl: "Well, you should have known about it, I sent you a memo."

It is also useful if you want to convince colleagues of your staggering burden of responsibility. Outlining your achievements in the last six months, you send a memo from yourself to yourself, but the latter is buried so deep in "cc." to other people that people are merely impressed and never realise to whom the memo is really being sent. The memo is also a status symbol. When people feel their position is really secure in a firm, they get their own memos printed: "From the pen (or the desk) of Caroline Nitwit-Thompson."

Such pomposity should not go unchallenged. Fire

back a memo: "From the occasional table of J. Cooper."
The memo of course is one of the strongest weapons
wielded by Miss Hitler from Personnel, who will fire
them off if someone is too prodigal with the guillotine,
or uses office elastic bands to hold her (or his) hair
back, or arrives a minute late in the morning.

Memos from the Managing Director should be read
before you make a paper dart out of them. Memos from
the legal department should also be taken seriously or
you may end up in gaol.

My favourite memo, however, was sent out by the
Media department of a big advertising agency: *"The
Muckshifter and Loader* has changed its name to *The
Muckshifter."*

MEETINGS

"The only meetings I like are between two people."

                                    Tennessee Williams.

Another king-sized timewaster. Twenty-four people
half asleep round a table making indecisions that only
concern a couple of those present anyway. Meetings,
however, are rather like cocktail parties. You don't
want to go, but you're cross not to be asked. They are
usually called by one person: the Sales Manager or
the Marketing Manager because–reluctant to act on
his own initiative–he wants official sanction for his
projects. Rising executives often call meetings to make
themselves feel important. A lot of meetings are held
to arrange when to have meetings.

Your certified rat will call meetings at 9.00 and 2.00 so
everyone arrives late, and it puts him one up.

Meetings today are usually called conferences to
make them sound more significant. Sales conferences
in particular are a nightmare. All that ghastly ra-rahing
and team rallying. A complete monologue from

The only meetings I like

the Managing Director punctuated by sycophantic laughter from the floor. It's rather like the end of term prize-giving, but unfortunately no one's going home for the holidays at the end of it.

Afterwards you have to attend a ghastly tea to meet the "reps", hideous heartiness prevails, bonhomie cubed, no one acts normally, everyone makes thumbs up signs to one another, and when you shake hands with someone you clasp his hand in both of yours.

In spite of all the rubbish talked about the miracle of the group think, new ideas very seldom emerge at meetings. If you've got a good idea, you're either too shy to produce it, or you keep it to yourself because you know it will be shot down or pinched by someone else.

A FEW TIPS

Save all your bad ideas for meetings. They'll be shot down, but you'll give the impression of being a bright young man.

If the meeting is going against you, steer the discussion round to cricket, which will hold up the proceedings for at least five minutes.

A good clash of wills stops everyone going to sleep. Argue ferociously against any ideas you secretly know are directly opposed to those of the Managing Director.

Combat sleep by deciding in order which people in the room you would most like to sleep with. Think what kind of animal they most resemble, and count the number of times a particular word like feasible, valuable, or meaningful is used.

If a rival of yours seems to be talking too persuasively and too long, distract everyone's attention by drawing a nude on your scribbling pad and reaching strategic parts of her anatomy as he is making his most telling points.

A rival talking too persuasively

One woman I knew used to smoke a pipe, and when she wanted to create a diversion she would get up,

wander down the table taking butts out of the ashtrays, tear them open and fill her pipe with the
tobacco.

Extra-mural activities

A lot of your working day will be spent out of the
office:

THE LUNCH HOUR
*Never drink black coffee at lunch; it will keep you awake
in the afternoon.*
Euphemistically called the lunch hour, this interval
in the day's inactivities runs from twelve to three-
thirty. This is the Piggies' High Noon when, snorting
with delight, they pour out of their offices like their
Gadarene forbears into the café opposite where they
eat three courses of soup, shepherd's pie and chips,
and treacle pudding followed by white coffee, after
which they waddle back to their office to eat biscuits
all afternoon.

The sekketries will reach peak activity during the
lunch hour, when they hare round doing their shopping, getting clothes out of the dry cleaners and
having their hair done. They also squeeze in three-
quarters of an hour to have lunch, sitting in each
other's laps in steamy coffee bars, fat girls eating
salads, thin girls eating spaghetti, their dissection of
last night's escapade only interrupted by the hiss of
the espresso machine.

Invariably just as they're getting down to a good bitch
about the office, they feel a heavy hand on their
shoulder; it will be Miss Hitler from Personnel asking
if she can join them.

Office Crones seldom go to lunch, but spend their hour
brewing tomato soup in the basement (or, because

A heavy hand on their shoulder

they're on a diet, sourly nibbling at cottage cheese and a piece of celery), adding another two rows to their green open-work jersey, and waiting to tear latecomers limb from limb.

Then, of course, there's the office canteen, with its menu improperly typed by one of the sekketries.

> Clean Soup
> Boiled button
> Stewed rears and naked egg custard.

Unless you want fat meat or the boniest piece of the fish, it's essential to waste a great deal of time chatting up the woman who runs the canteen. (She's the only woman in whom the Piggies display any interest.)

Meanwhile the directors are roughing it at the Ritz.

If you are to get on as an executive, you must realise that in order to do business with anyone, you must down two large pink gins, a three-course lunch with a good bottle of claret, and two double brandies, not forgetting cigars, at every stage of the deal.

How well I remember those nightmarish business lunches when I was a very junior Public Relations executive, entertaining lady journalists and wondering desperately what would be the right moment to tell them about the product I was supposed to be trying to flog.

Usually I funked it until the coffee stage, then said timidly, "Well-er about these fascinating rubber gloves." And the lady journalist would glance at her watch, mutter about a deadline, leap to her feet, thanking me profusely for a divine lunch, and disappear double quick out of the restaurant...

It always seems a slight anomaly that managements expect their executives to spend at least a tenner a day on lunch, then only issue the rest of the staff with 15p luncheon vouchers. I suppose this ensures wakefulness in the afternoon. No one could sleep on a 15p lunch.

A friendly grocer will usually exchange your vouchers for groceries. I used to buy cigarettes with mine.

LUNGE HOUR

The lunch hour is invariably followed by the lunge hour. This is the period of rocketing libidos and octopus hands, when bosses and executives return from lunch swollen with insolence and wine, and make passes at their sekketries and any pretty girls who seem to be around.

SKIVING

Thou shalt not kill time—shirkers of the world, unite.

It never hurts of course to put in an occasional

appearance in the office if only to make a few private calls, put your personal letters through the franking machine, and collect your expenses before going to lunch.

When I worked in an office, I was past-mistress at the art of skiving. I always used to arrange to see someone at 10.30 (which meant I needn't go into the office beforehand) and to deliver something by taxi at five o'clock (which meant I could take the taxi on home afterwards and charge it up on expenses).

One ploy – if you're very late in the morning – is to take off your coat and hide it, with your shopping bag, in a chum's office, then wander into your own, giving your boss the impression you've been in for hours discussing affairs of state on the directors' floor.

When you get back very late from lunch, distract people by bringing back a Fuller's cake to be shared round, or a pair of gardening gloves for the Office Crone.

Getting out in the middle of the afternoon or the morning is more tricky. Try walking out or in with a large package under your arm, or pretend to be very religious. In one office where I worked, one of the copywriters was always wandering up to our woman boss and saying in an unctuous whisper: "It's a saint's day. I'm just nipping off to church, if you don't mind." She could then stay away anything up to four hours – it was only regarded as proof of her devotion. You can also say you're Jewish, which means lots of days off.

Creative people can perpetuate the myth that they work better at home because it's quieter, and then push off to the cinema. If you are "working at home", it's always a good idea to ring in from time to time and sound very businesslike.

Another excellent ruse is to ring up and say you're taking a day's holiday and won't be in. Personnel never check up. One colleague of mine took 40 days' holiday in a year as well as his official three weeks.

Or you can establish a reputation for being delicate—a dicky heart, a bad back—then if you don't come in people will assume it's playing up.

A reputation for being delicate

Never take more than three days off, or you'll be involved in dreary wrangles over doctor's certificates. It's also important to look very ill when you return bravely to work on the fourth day.

I perfected a "sickly looking" make-up which fooled everyone. Very pale foundation, green face powder to give you a livid look, brown mascara smudged under the eyes, and, most important of all, a touch of pink lipstick rubbed into the eyelids, accompanied by a stoical expression.

Ten to one you'll look so ill they'll send you home after lunch for another three days' holiday.

One company, conscious of the degree of absenteeism, sent round a memo to all staff headed *Loafing*, attacking the practice of slipping out for a couple of hours in the afternoon on the pretext of buying a loaf of bread.

HOLIDAYS

At the first pallid shaft of January sunlight, typists will plunge into cotton dresses, baring their grey arms and freckled bosoms to the world, and Miss Hitler from Personnel will issue the holiday list. Within ten days she will descend on you and give you a rocket for not making up your mind when you want to go.

Bosses are hell

Other heinous crimes (apart from not planning your holiday in January) include not looking forward to it with feverish enthusiasm, and not sending a postcard when you get there wishing quite untruthfully that the whole of the typing pool were with you.

As weeks pass, these postcards are sellotaped on the side of the filing cabinet, like swastikas on Spitfires, alongside the pin-up photographs of Robert Redford and James Hunt.

Bosses are hell after they come back from holiday or long business trips. They feel guilty about skiving and spending too much of the firm's money on trips to the game reserves or geisha girls, and assuage their guilt by having efficiency drives and finding fault with everything you've done right during their absence. The sekketry should pander to her boss's feelings, make a few minor but obvious mistakes for him to discover so he can feel that the wheels do not run completely smoothly without him. She should say she's pleased he's back, even if she's not. Everyone likes to feel missed.

Visitors

Occasionally in offices you will have visitors. The temporary secretary, for example.

THE TEMPORARY
"I spent a week in Production, a week in the Art Department, a week in Control, a week out of control."
Every office should invest in a temporary at least twice a year to act as office scapegoat, then she can be blamed for every misdemeanour uncovered in the next six months.

58

A letter, for example, that never reaches its destination? The temporary must have written the wrong address. Chewing gum parked beneath the boardroom table? That must have been when the temporary took the minutes. The failure of the roller towel in the Ladies? Certainly the temporary's fault—she spent enough time in there doing her face.

On one occasion when I did a stint of temporary typing I worked for some engineers who kicked me out when I got the giggles over a memo consigning: "four hundred eccentric nipples to Rotterdam." I won't elaborate on the week I spent at the Mechanical Handling Exhibition, except to say the handling I received was far from mechanical.

I also managed to last three weeks in an insurance company because I pretended I had a title which impressed them. The typing pool was run by a Crone who bullied us all unmercifully. One day she went to the dentist to get her fangs fixed, and the girl sitting next to me asked me if I'd like to have a look at the Crone's secret book.

It was hidden in her bottom drawer under packets of squashed flies: a book of animal photographs, and beneath each photograph she had pencilled in faintly the name of a member of the firm. Beside a row of pigs were four members of the Claims Department, beside an evil-looking warthog, the Personnel Officer, beside a sloth, the most idle member of the Pool.

"Oh look, she's added a new one," said my friend.

There, beside a picture of a white rat with terrified eyes running round a treadmill, she had written: Jilly Cooper.

The unkindest cut of all, however, was when the agency sent me to a nursing organization staffed almost entirely by women. In actual fact I and two male nurses were the only "women" in the place. Time and again I was pounced upon by Amazon after

Won't you become permanent, my dear?

Amazon in the canteen, under the desk, behind the filing cabinet. At last I heard those longed-for bass-baritone words: "Won't you become permanent, my dear?"

THE COMPUTER

"Our daily sales are now done by a commuter."

The computer was originally brought in as a high-salaried whizz kid, who made all the staff very edgy and worried about their jobs. Now they realise its limitations they are no longer worried. The computer lies exhausted in the basement, its digits set at 000000000000. There has been a computer pogrom. No one knows what to do with it. It is not even allowed to pay salaries, as they're considered too confidential. It is inclined to pay people twice for work they haven't done. Its mistakes are sorted out by some undiplomatic bag in a grey dress.

It first disgraced itself because it sent 100 books to the West Indies instead of W.1. London.

All the departments that were abolished when the computer was installed are now creeping back under new names like Data Control and Central Control, and are staffed largely by temporaries.

Finally, an even more unwelcome but more frequent guest is the management consultant.

MANAGEMENT CONSULTANTS

Management consultants waste time, cost money, make the staff twitchy and are probably working for competitors. If by any chance your office is unfortunate enough to suffer a plague of them, there are certain tactics that can be employed. Always tell lies when they ask you questions about your work, by saying that everything takes you twice as long as it really does. Tell them the most horrifying stories about your superiors, but above all tell them how out-of-date and appallingly maintained every piece of office equipment is—and hint that the management are so at each other's throats that the only way of saving the firm is by removing practically every member of the board.

This not only gives you the faint hope of a better job yourself, but will be a distinct spur to the management consultant to create a plum job for himself. (Although they're not allowed to do this, we all know that they do.)

They will then introduce vast quantities of new office equipment (they're probably on a cut from the manufacturers) and will replace half the staff, but it will be necessary later to employ an entirely new set of people to maintain, manage and operate the equipment. These people will always command higher salaries than the ones the machinery replaced, thus the cost of them, plus the cost of the machinery, plus the management consultants' fee, coupled with the inevitable losses incurred by decreased efficiency all round, mean that the company is invariably far worse off than it was before.

I can only add an instance when the management consultants moved in on a symphony concert. Here are some of their findings:

"For considerable periods, the four oboe players had nothing to do. The number should be reduced and the work spread more evenly over the whole orchestra, thus eliminating peaks of activity."

"No useful purpose is served by repeating on the horns a passage that has already been played on the strings."

"All twelve of the violins played identical notes. The staff of this section should be drastically cut. It is estimated that if all the redundant passages were eliminated the whole concert time could be reduced to twenty minutes and there would be no need for an interval."

Office pastimes

BOREDOM

In any office you will have long passages of boredom. When I shared an office with a colleague we used to take it in turns to go through the telephone lists, pick out two people e.g. the Office Crone and Miss Hitler from Personnel, and say: "Which one would you rather go to bed with?" The other person had to make a snap decision before you counted five.

A great deal of the typists' time will be spent speculating about the lovelife of other members of the staff.

"She'd be quite attractive if she made more of herself," they agree, "but she ought to go on a diet" (which means she'll presumably make less of herself.

Miss Taylor in Accounts

Confusing?). Or they will discuss Miss Taylor in Accounts who's so very "refined and smart" they can't see why she isn't married.

On an executive level, the day will be passed discussing the respective merits of different hedge-clippers and insulation materials, talking about the greenhouse you are going to put up in the garden next week when you've finished wall-papering the dog's kennel, and telling your colleagues how you make home-made wine.

Grumbling is also a great time-waster. Listen politely to other people's moans, but never offer to help them out. We all know the moaner who spends all morning tearing his hair over his workload, and telling you he's heading for a crack-up. So you offer to do some of his work for him. He accepts with alacrity; the crack-up is halted in mid-stream. He will then go to lunch, and ring in about 3.30 to say he's a bit tied up and won't be back. Next morning he'll come staggering in and moaning once more about his workload.

SEX IN THE OFFICE

Dear Sir Stroke Madam

Offices vary: some are like monasteries, and the only thing you're likely to get raped by is the spacebar on the long-carriage typewriter. Others out-thrum *Peyton Place*. As an ex-colleague said: "You have to knock on people's office doors before you go in, not out of courtesy, just to give them time to get their trousers up."

There's certainly nothing like the odd pass to lighten the tedium of office life, nor the odd crush on your boss to make you look forward to Monday morning instead of dreading it.

You'll find too that the Personnel Lady and Judy O'Grady are nymphos under the skin. As soon as a new Adonis joins the firm, the Office Crones start dunking themselves in Devon Violets, the typing pool turn their skirts up to groin level with the office stapler, and even the senior sekketries treat themselves to a home perm and set the directors' floor throbbing with middle-aged desire.

In my experience, sex in the office is catching like the measles. Once one director discovers another director is knocking off his sekketry he starts wondering why he shouldn't have a bit on the side as well, and lust is transmitted down the hierarchy. When you consider that a boss spends more of his waking life with his sekketry than with his wife, it's hardly surprising that accidents happen.

Another contributing factor is that most women are attracted by power, and absolute power attracts absolutely. Thus the most grey, sexless men take on a lustre when they assume the mantle of Managing Director or head of the department. All women want

The most grey, sexless men

to play Egeria, but on the other hand they are seldom drawn to subordinates. I don't think Lady Chatterley's Office Boy is a viable proposition.

I think there should be lots of pretty girls in the office too. It cheers the men up if they can wolf-whistle while they work.

Some people are very clever at concealing the fact that they are having an affair with someone in the office. One woman executive I'd always thought was a pillar of respectability told me long after I'd left the firm that she'd been to bed with three members of the board in the same day: one first thing in the morning (he'd been spending the night with her), the second she took home to lunch, and the third had her for supper.

Usually, however, the couple having a walk-out congratulate themselves on being terribly discreet, carefully leaving the office at different times, meeting half-a-mile down the road and ostentatiously not speaking to each other when they meet in the passage. When in fact the forked tongues have been wagging for weeks and the whole of the building has been watching the affaire develop with passionate interest.

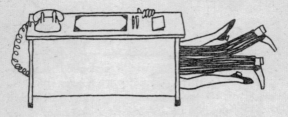

There are certain ways of telling

There are certain ways, too, of telling if your boss is having an affaire with someone:

If he starts getting in when the dew is still on the filing cabinets, and you're knocked sideways by the smell of *Brut for Men*.

If he keeps getting calls on the internal telephone and makes ambiguous remarks into it: "We must play this one very close to the chest, we'd better thrash the whole problem of production out over lunch. How about Overton's at 1 o'clock?"

If he comes back after a three-hour lunch ostensibly with a client, and immediately sends you out for sandwiches, or yawns his head off and spends the afternoon loudly rustling papers to disguise the fact that his stomach is rumbling.

If he and Miss Nitwit-Thompson both disappear individually but at the same time to buy the evening paper, stay away for an hour and return having forgotten to buy it.

If he and Miss Nitwit-Thompson both ring in to say they're ill with gastro-enteritis.

If he's having an affaire with someone outside the office, he'll get lots of handwritten letters marked Private and Confidential which he'll rush off to the loo to read.

DIRECT MALES

If, on the other hand, you've got designs on him yourself, your best bet will be to wait for the office party rather than the office dance, when he will be inhibited by the presence of his wife. Be careful, though. The lust that raged in his bosom on Christmas Eve can easily evaporate, and when he comes back to the office after the holiday, those burst balloons all over the floor and the fly floating in a glass of sherry on his desk may be too much for him, and he'll decide to dispense with your services altogether.

If the office wolf – who's always been a gentleman to his fingertips where you're concerned – suddenly becomes a gentleman only to his wrists and starts molesting you at every opportunity, don't slap his face (there's no point in making enemies) but tell him about your new boy friend, who's a black belt at judo and so jealous of other men he's inclined to beat them into a pulp.

If you've got your eye on one of those rising young bachelors, just say you're related to the Managing Director. You'll soon find those indecent proposals become decent ones.

If, on the other hand, you are a rising young bachelor and you want to keep the typing pool at bay, get a photograph of somebody's wife and children and put it in a leather frame on your desk.

Nor will you find it difficult to tell if one of the typists gets a crush on you. Not only will she wear her heart picked out in da-glo on her sleeve, she will also not join the general exodus at 5 p.m. but hang about waiting to be asked out for a drink. She will also make

A rising young bachelor

every possible excuse to come into your office, bringing in the morning mail one letter at a time, then coming in first with your tea, then the milk, then the sugar, then the teaspoon.

If you are an Adonis, scuffles will break out in the passage over which of the typing pool is to bring in your tea. Potted plants will bloom on your window ledge, giggling will follow you down the passage, and you will have your letters typed quicker and better than anyone else in the building.

If you want these attentions to continue, steer clear of the lot of them. Once you settle for one girl, the rest of the pool will lose interest and transfer their affections to the newly arrived Eminence Grease with the good desk-side manner.

If you fall in love with the girl, neither of you will get any work done. She will very likely take advantage of the situation and become insubordinate, lazy and forgetful. Once you get bored with her, you'll be in real trouble, for she'll be snivelling into a damp Kleenex all day and commuting back and forth to the loo. Your potted plants will wither, and the rest of the pool will mutter and glare at you. There's no divorce in the office. Death or giving in your notice is the only thing that will part you.

Finally, if you do get really keen on someone in the office, before doing anything rash like proposing marriage, get another job and see your beloved in perspective. Find out if you've got anything in common besides talking shop and evading the Office Crone, or if it was merely the fascination of the clandestine that gave an edge to the affaire.

OFFICE POLITICS

The trouble with this sinking ship is that all the rats are staying.

Apart from making and evading passes, eighty per cent of your time in any office will be spent in the area of competition: playing the power game and jockeying for position. Executives will go round after dark emptying your wastepaper basket and piecing your confidential memos together. Every time you go down the passage you'll be subjected to a party political broadcast on behalf of the Accounts Department.

Feuding goes on between person and person, and between departments, who will all try to shift blame onto each other. The Publicity Department, for example, will drive other departments into a frenzy of rage, merely because they make more noise and appear to do less work than anyone else, and consider the fact that they work late occasionally on a press party gives them the excuse to swan in late every day. The Personnel and the Accounts Departments fight with everyone. Even the Sales Department will be in a state of constant warfare with the warehouse.

Lunch at a five-star restaurant

As a young executive, sooner or later one of the
directors will ask you out to lunch at a five-star
restaurant. When you get to the swirling brandy stage
he will start rhubarbing about getting the dead man's
hand off the wheel, and then offer you a junior ministry
in his Shadow Cabinet.

Don't commit yourself to joining his faction, just say
you absolutely see his point. And don't let him see you
going out with his rival director to another five-star
lunch the next day.

Your real office Machiavelli, however, will place his
own men in key positions throughout the firm and
then set up:

THE PALACE REVOLUTION

A palace revolution will be heralded by the following
signs:

Various top brass will start getting in unusually early in the morning, and stand about in the corridors whispering. Directors who are known to loathe each other start going out to lunch together. Strange files are suddenly sent for, urgent calls are made to the firm's accountants or solicitors from directors who normally don't deal with them. A publicity handout is run off in conditions of great secrecy and circulated to the press, who are told to treat the matter in confidence and not to release the news until they get the O.K. from the Deputy Managing Director's sekketry. The Deputy Managing Director having set the whole thing up, flies to Hamburg to see a client and waits to see what happens.

If the Managing Director is overthrown by the rest of the Board, the Deputy Managing Director will fly back and take over. If not he will deny all knowledge of the conspiracy.

The Piggies will take absolutely no notice and go to lunch.

Supplementing your income

If you work in an office there are three main ways of supplementing your income: expenses, moonlighting and getting a rise.

EXPENSES

> In Bradford, she was Mabel,
> She was Margery in Perth,
> In Plymouth, she was Phoebe,
> The sweetest girl on earth.
> In London she was Doris,
> The cutest of the bunch.
> But down on his expenses
> They were petrol, oil and lunch.

The first essential is to make friends with the cashier—he can make things very difficult if he wants to. The second is to hand in your expenses at least once if not twice a week. They always seem more credible if you present them little and often.

Cooking one's expenses is an art. In one job in which I worked we used to set at least one day a week aside for the purpose, and the manager, who never stirred from the office, used to put in a regular weekly bill for £25.

And one journalist I heard of recently, who had drawn advance expenses of over £1,500, appeared to be in such a muddle over them that he was given a fortnight's holiday to sort them out. Like the Evelyn Waugh journalist who charged up £300 for camels when he was abroad.

Expenses of course are not what they used to be. You can't charge up £20 for fictitious lunches any more—you have to produce bills in evidence. Ask all your friends to save their bills for you; and you can of course always come to some arrangement with the local restaurateur—he gives you a sheaf of other people's bills, and you continue to patronise his restaurant. If the bill is outlandish, always say you were lunching a foreigner, then it can be set against tax.

You can also:

Travel by bus and charge up for a taxi.

Travel third class and charge up for first class.

Swim the Atlantic and charge up for the airfare.

A "round of drinks for information gained" is always good for a fiver.

"Cloakroom and gratuities" will pull in £1 every time.

MOONLIGHTING

Moonlighting means working for two different firms at once, and earning two salaries. This is best achieved by slipping into one of those pockets of inefficiency in a big firm where you've plenty of spare time on your hands.

I've moonlighted most of my working career. It began when I joined a large firm of publishers and, realising there wasn't enough work for me, I got another job as a fiction editor on a magazine. It was a full-time job, but then I had a typewriter, a sekketry, a telephone and a post-room to handle all the mail.

I used to reach the office at 8.30 every morning, and rattle away at my fiction editing. Everyone in the publishing firm thought I was working like a slave—so they left me alone. I used to claim expenses from both jobs, and my cup was full when I got rises from both companies at Christmas.

Occasionally there were complications when both jobs got busy simultaneously, and telephone calls came through on the publisher's switchboard asking for me as the fiction editor. I used to feel a bit like a man with a wife and a mistress who were both complaining he wasn't paying them enough attention.

My favourite moonlighter was a girl who joined one of my previous firms as a sekketry. Peculiar men kept ringing her up, and she was always slipping out of the office for four-hour lunches. Eventually after six months we discovered she was working as a prostitute on the side.

Another way you can supplement your income is to ask for a rise.

HOW TO GET A RISE OUT OF SOMEONE

Go to your boss and say you've been offered a fabulous job, you don't want to take it but with a wife and six parrots to support you've simply got to think of their interests first. If you're any good they'll give you a rise to keep you.

Beware, though. I heard the other day of a man who

tried precisely this tactic:

Him: I've been offered this fabulous job etc.

Boss: Good for you. You had better take it then, hadn't you? When do you start?

Exit friend jobless and speechless.

You can also borrow so much money from the firm on a paying-back basis that they've got to give you a rise ever to get their money back.

Borrow a pregnant lady

Or invite your pregnant wife or borrow a pregnant lady and parade her up and down as often as you can in the office in gym shoes with holes in, and keep a photograph of seven children on your desk (you can always get such photographs from agencies).

The logical way of course is to work harder, but make

sure everyone realises it.

In one firm, one of the junior sekketries typed the following letter to the Managing Director:

"Dear Sir,

I would like to thank you for my rise of £1. I will do my bust to justify your faith in me."

HOW NOT TO GIVE SOMEONE A RISE

Miss Nitwit-Thompson asks for a rise.

Send for her, get out a file which says *Nitwit-Thompson, Confidential* and leave it in a prominent position on your desk. Don't look up for five minutes when she comes into your office. Then ask her to sit down, and flip meditatively through her confidential file, frowning a great deal.

Look up and say: "We're very overloaded with deadwood in this firm, you know." (Long pause to make her jumpy.) "We've got to hack it out before we can give anyone a rise."

Then get out a very complicated chart with everyone's salary on it, look at it for a few minutes, then say: "You're getting a great deal more than anyone else your age. I wonder how that came about?" (Another long pause.)

And Miss Nitwit-Thompson slinks out of your office terrified you're going to dock her wages.

Other ways you can avoid giving someone a rise include:

Praising their work inordinately and promoting them to something meaningless like: Special Director or Deputy Assistant to the Personnel Manager.

Giving them more responsibility.

Offering to have their offices painted for them.

Upgrading their company car from an 1100 to an 1800 — in the figures lies the deceit. They can then say they've got a rise of 700 and forget to mention the cc's.

The firing squad

The management of a large agency decided overnight to axe 80 per cent of their creative staff and hired a hatchet man to fire them in triplicate. After he'd finished his dirty work, they fired him as well.

If a boss is unsatisfied with the work of a member of his staff, he should send for him, find out whether his inefficiency is due to family trouble, sickness etc. and if not, give him a rocket and warn him that unless he improves radically he will be given a month's notice at the end of the month. Too many bosses sack their staff without giving them a chance to do better, or without them realising their work is unsatisfactory.

Even more insidious is the freezing out method practised by managements who will do anything to avoid a direct confrontation.

The procedure is as follows:

Stage One: You are suddenly no longer asked to meetings or 'cc'ed on memos, your name is removed from the magazine circulation list, people stop talking as you walk down the passage. Your sekketry starts forgetting to water your plants and spends her time taking letters from the newly arrived whizz-kid/certified rat, who's currently working in the passage outside your office.

Stage Two: As your paranoia intensifies, you are given less and less to do and office juniors start cheeking you, until . . .

Stage Three: You arrive on Monday morning to find the whizz kid installed in your office, his name beside yours on the door. During the week his furniture is moved in until you're both perching on top of the filing cabinet.

Stage Four: You turn up the following Monday to find your desk in the passage, so, self-respect in tatters, you finally get the message and start looking for another job.

If you're under contract it's more tricky for them to boot you out, but they get round it by transferring you to outer Alaska at a vastly reduced salary and refusing to pay your wife and parrot's fare.

Another ruse is to wait until you go on holiday. You stagger in from the beach too blinded at first by the sun to read the registered letter bidding you take your disservices somewhere else.

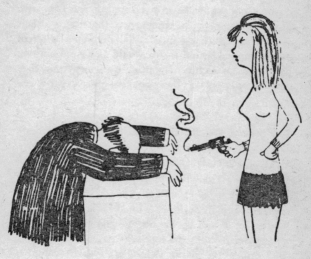

Turn the tables

Of course there are numerous things you can do to turn the tables on the people who've sacked you—like Napoleon's Finance Minister, who crippled the country's entire monetary system by retiring into his office for three days and burning every document he could lay his hands on. Or the man in the sweet factory who wrote four-letter words instead of "Welcome to Blackpool" in the inside of half a mile of rock.

Some people avenge themselves by spending their last month appropriating office property: writing paper, sugar, paper clips, elastic bands. A man I know completely equipped his new flat with office furniture. One evening when he was struggling out of the building with a bookcase he met the chairman, who did not realise it was company property and gave him a helping hand to the car.

N.B. Sometimes–even if you know you're for the chop–it's a good idea to hang on. In one firm, two directors came to the conclusion that one of their executives was useless and decided to fire him. Both of them assumed the other one would do it, and nothing happened for eighteen months, by which time they decided he could stay on as he'd got more experience.

Social occasions

THE OFFICE OUTING

Whether it's *Tulip Time in Spalding, Lincs.*, *A Charity Walk to Gravesend* or *A Night out in London's Theatre-land*, this beastly romp is loathed both by the people who go on it, and by the people who organise it. It's a hangover from feudal forelock-tugging times, when the Lords of the Manor used to give charity banquets for the poor. It should be abolished and the money spent on extra bonuses.

THE LEAVING PARTY

In some offices, there's a permanent round of parties after work. Either you're celebrating landing a big contract, or cheering each other up for losing it, or saying good-bye to someone, or wishing them happy birthday, or celebrating the fact that their cat's just had kittens.

Leaving parties are occasions when sex rears its ugly head, for while you are saying good-bye to dear old Fothers from Production who's been with the firm for forty years, you will probably drink enough to say a big hello to Miss Twink from the typing pool, whose knickers are bursting into flames at the thought of you.

Hardly a day passes either without some office junior coming round waving a manilla envelope collecting for someone's birthday or leaving present–executives will be considered very mean if they give less than 50p, and directors must give at least £1. Later in the day you will have to add your name at an acute angle to a myriad others on a leaving card. It is interesting to note how much more talent and imagination manifests itself in leaving cards than in any other project produced by the art or copy departments; it is the one example of work that is not fettered by red tape or mucked about by senior members of the hierarchy.

THE OFFICE DANCE

Another beastly romp. Attendance is usually "optional", but it's frowned upon if you don't turn up. All the warehouse comes up for the evening, their wives with sequinned hair and fat shoulders bulging over strapless satin. The office slut who's been slopping around all year in bedroom slippers, her dyed orange hair going black at the roots, immediately turns into a swan and hooks half the men in the room.

You are expected to sit down to a five-course dinner at five o'clock in the evening when no one's at all hungry except the Piggies.

The seating plan is devised by some sadist in the

basement who sees that you are not placed next to anyone you know, so you exchange platitudes with some Latvian packer's wife, as you plough valiantly through lumps of sole and bombes surprises, then have to listen to inaudible speeches.

Afterwards the high and mighty unbend enough to dance and there are Paul Joneses which turn into a rugger scrum because all the typing pool are fighting tooth and nail to end up opposite the office Adonis.

Always dance with the boss's wife—she is officially your hostess.

Always dance with the senior sekketries and your own sekketry.

Be careful not to beat the directors at musical chairs— one man who did, sank without trace in the New Year. Let them win all the spot prizes.

Bar propping is, alas, much disapproved of.

Look cheerful, stay vertical. The opportunists will be out in force giving the impression they are having the night of their lives, and being seen by the Managing Director to be good mixers.

The only interest lies in seeing members of the staff's wives and husbands for the first time. Who would have thought mildewed Mr Meed from Packaging would turn up with such a corker? And Mrs Higgins from Production has always left early on the grounds that her husband beats her up if she's not home by six to give him his tea. He turns out to be half her size with thinning hair and a stutter.

THE CHRISTMAS PARTY

Finally there's the Office Christmas Party—subtly different from the Office Dance, because no wives or husbands or lovers are invited to inhibit the fun.

This is a typical office party:

It's Christmas Eve in the workhouse. The typing pool has been transformed into a fairy grotto. The typists are red-faced from the hairdresser's and blowing up balloons—they have been making furtive trips to the Ladies all afternoon to see if their dresses have hung out properly. Excitement seethes. This is the night when supertax husbands are hooked. In other parts of the building the higher echelons anticipate the evening with trepidation and veiled lust. The building already reverberates with revelry. The Art Department, having declared U.D.I., held their party before midday and are still going strong.

At 4.55, when it's too late to rush out and get her something, the Office Crone makes everyone feel a louse by handing out gaily wrapped presents. At 5.00 everyone stops typing in mid-word and thunders down to the Ladies which soon resembles the changing room at The Way In. The office junior has used hair lacquer under her arms instead of deodorant and is walking round like a penguin.

The party begins with everyone standing under the fluorescent lighting wondering what to say next—strange, considering they find no difficulty during working hours. Miss Nitwit-Thompson, who has been putting her Christmas cards through the franking machine all afternoon and telephoning her friends to say what a bore the party is going to be, has not bothered to change out of her grey jersey dress. She will be leaving after five minutes to catch a train home to Daddy.

In an attempt to please everyone, the £80 collected for drink has been spent on one bottle of everything from Brown Ale to Babycham. The caretaker who is manning the bar has assembled a strange collection of glasses: flower vases, toothmugs, bakelite cups. The Office Wolf is busy lacing the typists' orange juice with vodka.

Neatly displayed in out-trays is food cooked by members of the staff; curling sandwiches, flaccid

81

cheese straws with baker's droop, and an aggressive-looking Christmas cake covered in festive robins baked by the Office Crone. The Piggies have already got their heads down in the trough.

Conversation is still laboured, but the arrival of the Production department, who've been boozing all day on free liquor, helps to jolly things along. Soon, members of the Board drift down from Olympus, genial from a succession of long Christmas lunches.

The Receptionist, who is not famed for the strength of her knicker elastic, is making a very alive set at the handsome director of Public Relations. Miss Nitwit-Thompson discovers she's met the Managing Director's son at a number of dinner parties Soon they are nose to nose.

People are relaxing. Someone puts on a record and two typists dance together. One of the young men on the make is overheard boasting about his expenses by the Financial Director and loses his chance of promotion. The office cat has wriggled out of his green Xmas bow and is thoughtfully licking fish paste out of the sandwiches.

Faces are reddening, backs are being slapped, people are passing round packets of fifty cigarettes. The Managing Director needs little encouragement to get up and say what a big happy family they all are.

The Office Junior swells with pride at the thought that she and about 400 other people are entirely responsible for the firm's turnover. The caretaker takes the opportunity to rinse some glasses in the fire bucket.

A packer arrives from the warehouse with shiny blue suit and horny hands, and claims a dance with one of the senior sekketries, who bends over backwards to avoid his four-ale breath. The Receptionist and the Director of Public Relations are having private relations behind the filing cabinet.

The Managing Director's wife, who has come to

Claims a dance with a senior sekketry

collect her husband, has taken a piece of Christmas cake in deference to the typing pool. She didn't realise the robins were made of plaster, and is now desperately trying to spit out a beak.

Lust is rising in the vast jacked-up bosom of Miss Hitler from Personnel, and she is jostling the newest trainee towards the mistletoe. The Office Boy has hiccups and is trying to roll cheese and chutney sandwiches into an electric typewriter.

"God bless you all, Merry Christmas," cries the departing Managing Director.

Now he's gone the fun is unconfined. There is a general unfastening of chastity belts. The Sales Director is playing bears round the furniture, the Office Wolf

Lust is rising

keeps turning off the lights. Squeaks and scuffles break out in nearby offices. The oldest member of the staff is telling anyone who will listen how the firm grew from a tiny two-room business to the "great concern we are today". The Director of Public Relations is in the Gents desperately scrubbing lipstick from his shirt front.

The drink has run out. Miss Nitwit-Thompson, who is now quite giggly, is being taken to Annabels by the Managing Director's son. She'll be lucky if she gets home to Daddy before Boxing Day.

Reluctant to end the evening, people are making plans

to meet in pubs or the backs of cars. Others are saying "Merry Christmas", exchanging beery kisses and taking uncertain steps towards the nearest bus stop.

The caretaker, who has appropriated several bottles of drink, shakes his head over the pair of rose-pink pants in the Gents. Under a pile of forgotten coats and umbrellas lies a doll's tea set and a mournful-looking turkey. As he locks up, a telephone rings unaccountably in one of the lifts.

How to stay married

To Leo

introduction

It is extremely easy to get married—it costs £14·25 and takes three days to get a licence. It is much harder to stay married.

My only qualifications for writing a book on the subject are that I have had the example of parents who have lived in harmony for nearly fifty years, and I myself am still married extremely happily after fifteen years. In fifteen years, of course, we've had marvellous patches and patches so bad that they rocked our marriage to its foundations, but I've come to realise that if you can cling on like a barnacle during the bad patches, your marriage will survive and in all probability be strengthened.

Anyone else's marriage is a dark unexplored continent, and although I have observed far too many of my friends going swiftly in and out of wedlock, I can only guess at what it was that broke the marriage up. Since the word got around that I was writing this book, my task has been made doubly difficult by the fact that married couples either sidled away or started behaving ostentatiously well, whenever I came into the room.

One of the great comforts of my own marriage, however, has been that my husband was married before, knew the ropes, and during any really black period, when I was all for opting out and packing my bags, would reassure me that such black periods were to be expected in marriage, and it had been far worse for him the first time round.

Similarly I hope that by pointing out some of the disasters and problems that beset us and how we weathered them, it may reassure other people either married or contemplating marriage.

Here comes the bride

THE WEDDING

This is blast off—the day you (or rather your mother) have been waiting for all your life. It'll pass in a dream and afterwards you won't remember a thing about it. It helps, however, if you both turn up. Dope yourself with tranquillizers by all means, but watch the champagne later: drugs mixed with drink often put you out like a light. And don't forget to take the price tags off your new shoes, they'll show when you kneel down in church.

Brides: don't be disappointed if you don't look your best, far more likely you'll be scarlet in the face and piggy-eyed from lack of sleep.

Bride not looking her best

Bridegrooms: remember to look round and smile as your bride comes up the aisle. She'll be too busy coping with her bouquet and veil to notice, but it will impress those armies of guests lined up on either side of the church.

Groom smiling at bride

Coming down the aisle's more tricky – you never know where to look, that radiant smile can easily set into a rictus grin, and there's bound to be one guest you know too well, whose eye you want to avoid (like Tallulah Bankhead's remark about one couple coming down the aisle: "I've had them both and they were lousy!").

If you look solemn, people will think you're having second thoughts. Best policy is to settle for a cool smirk with your eyes on the door of the church.

Be careful what hymns you choose. People like a good bellow at a wedding, so don't choose anything obscure. Equally, be careful of hymns with double meanings like, "Jesu – the very thought of thee", which will make everyone giggle and spoil the dignity and repose of the occasion.

THE RECEPTION

First there's the line up, and you'll get so tired of shaking hands, trying to remember faces and gushing like an oil well, you'll begin to have a real sympathy for the Royal Family.

Don't worry when you circulate among the guests afterwards if none of them will speak to you. They'll all feel you're far too important to waste time talking to them, and you'll wander round like a couple of wraiths.

If you must make speeches, keep them short. Thank everyone in sight, and tell one stunning joke to convince your in-laws you do have a sense of humour after all. Never let the best man either speak or read the telegrams.

Don't flirt with exes. One girl I know, whose husband spent the reception playing 'do you remember' with an old girlfriend, refused to go on the honeymoon.

Try not to get drunk – you may feel like it – but it will cause recriminations later.

The Honeymoon

Originally, the honeymoon was intended for husbands to initiate their innocent young brides into the delights and mysteries of sex. Today, when most couples have slept together anyway and are already bankrupted by the cost of setting up house, the whole thing seems a bit of a farce and a needless expense. You probably both need a holiday, however.

When you arrive at your destination, you're likely to feel a sense of anti-climax. You're exhausted and suffering from post-champagne depression (a real killer). For months you've been coping with squabbles with the caterers, bridesmaids' tantrums over their head-dresses, parcels arriving every day, the hall littered with packing straw, writer's cramp from answering letters, traumas with the dressmakers – every moment's been occupied, you're wound up like a clock, and suddenly it's all over and you've nothing to do for a fortnight except each other.

For the wife in particular, everything's suddenly new and unfamiliar, her spongebag and flannel, new pigskin luggage, a whole trousseau of new clothes, dazzling white underwear instead of the usual dirty grey – even her name is new.

The thing to remember is that your wife/husband is probably as nervous and in need of reassurance as you are, like the wild beast surprised in the jungle who's always supposed to be more frightened than oneself.

SABOTEURS

The first thing to do on arrival at your honeymoon hotel is to search the bedroom for signs of sabotage. Jokey wedding guests may well have instructed the hotel staff to make you an apple pie bed, or wire up the springs of the bed to the hotel fire alarm.

One couple I know reached their hotel to be confronted by the manager waving a telegram from one such joker saying: "My wife has just run off with my best friend, I believe they are booked into your hotel under the assumed name of Mr. and Mrs. So and So. Could you refuse to let them have the booked room until I arrive." Whether you're heading for the Bahamas or Billericay, the best way to scotch honeymoon saboteurs is not to be coy about your destination. Simply tell everyone you're staying at the Grand and then book rooms at the Majestic.

Then there's the problem of getting used to living together. Here again the wife in particular will be worried about keeping up appearances. Before marriage she's relied on mud packs and rollers and skinfood at night, but now her husband's going to be with her every moment of the day, and the mystery's going to be ruined. When's she going to find time to shave her legs? And she's always told her husband she's a natural blonde, and suddenly he's going to find the home-bleacher in her suitcase.

She'll soon get used to it all, just as she'll get used to sitting on the loo and gossiping to her husband while he's having a bath, or to wandering around with nothing on instead of discreetly changing in the bathroom.

If she's ashamed of her small breasts and mottled thighs, he's probably equally self-conscious about his narrow shoulders and hairless chest.

If she's ashamed . . .

FIRST THING IN THE MORNING

If you're worried you look like a road accident in the mornings, sleep with the curtains drawn, and if you're scared your mouth will taste like a parrot's cage when he bends over to kiss you, pretend you're going to the loo, and nip out and clean your teeth.

DON'T PANIC if you get bored, or have a row, or feel claustrophobic or homesick. These are all part of growing-together pains. They won't establish a behaviour pattern for the next fifty years.

A vital honeymoon ploy is to go somewhere where there is plenty to do. It's not sacrilege to go to the cinema or watch a soccer match or even look up friends in the district. Take lots of books and sleeping pills.

DON'T PANIC if you get on each other's nerves. My mother, who's been happily married to my father for almost fifty years, nearly left him on honeymoon because he got a line of doggerel on his mind and repeated it over and over again as they motored through the cornfields of France.

We drove round Norfolk on our honeymoon and I nearly sent my husband insane by exclaiming: "How lovely", every time we passed a village church.

SEX

I'm not going into the intricacies of sexual initiation—there are numerous books on the subject—I would just plead for both parties to be patient, tolerant, appreciative and understanding. Temporary frigidity and impotence are not infrequent occurrences on honeymoon, and not to be taken too seriously.

Take things slowly, you've probably got a lifetime in front of you—all that matters at this stage is to get across strong that you love each other, and you're not sorry you are married.

DON'T WORRY if, unlike the girl in *The Carpetbaggers* who wanted to see nothing but ceilings on her honeymoon, you don't feel like leaping on each other all the time. As I've already pointed out, you're probably exhausted and in no condition for a sexual marathon.

Do take a red towel if you're a virgin, or likely to have the Curse. It saves embarrassment over the sheets.

Even if you've been sleeping together for ages beforehand, and sex was stunning, don't worry if it goes off for a bit, or feel convinced that it can only work in a clandestine setting. You haven't been married before, and may just be having initial panic because the stable door is well and truly bolted.

One friend told me he was woken up in the middle of most nights of his honeymoon by his wife staggering groggily out of bed, groping for her clothes and muttering she must get home before her parents woke up.

Eases tensions

It's a good idea to borrow someone's cottage in the country for a honeymoon. It's cheaper than an hotel, and you won't be worried by the imagined chortlings of chambermaids and hallporters, and you can cook if you get bored.

Don't worry if he/she doesn't gaze into your eyes all the time and quote poetry. Most people don't know enough poetry to last more than a quarter of an hour. A certain amount of alcohol is an excellent idea—it eases tension, breaks down inhibitions. Take the case of the girl in our office who on her arrival with her new husband at the hotel was presented with a bottle of champagne.

"It was wonderful," she told us. "We shared a glass each night and made the bottle last the whole fortnight."

WEDDING PRESENTS

Get your thank-you letters written before the wedding. Once the pre-wedding momentum has been lost, you'll never get down to them.

Don't beef too much about the presents your partner's family or friends have given you, even if they are ghastly. No one likes to be reminded that they are related to, or acquainted with, people of execrable taste. Try and keep a list of who gave you what, so you can bring those cake forks out of hiding when Aunt Agatha comes to tea, and you won't, as we did, give a particularly hideous vase back to the woman who gave it to us, when later she got married.

Setting up house

MOVING IN

At best a nightmare—as Dorothy Parker said, the one dependable law of life is that everything is always worse than you thought it was going to be.

When my parents moved into their first house, they arrived to find the electricians had all the floor boards up, the paint was wet in the kitchen, and there was an enormous pile of rubble in the garage surmounted by a one-horned, one-eyed stag.

Try therefore to get all major structural alterations done beforehand. Nothing is more depressing than trying to get a place straight with builders trooping in and out with muddy feet and demands for endless cups of tea. Even the smallest job will seem as though they're building the pyramids.

Try to get shelves up beforehand; removal men unpack at a fantastic rate, and you'll soon find every inch of floor space covered and nowhere to put anything. Don't forget to get the gas and electricity connected. Buy plenty of light bulbs.

Make a plan where everything is going—or you'll end up with the grand piano in the lavatory, the fridge in the bedroom, and two little removal men buckling under the sideboard while you have a ferocious argument where to put it.

Get some food in. You'll be so busy, you won't realise it's past 5.30, and the shops are shut, and you'll be so bankrupted tipping the removal men and rushing out to buy picture wire, screws and plugs, you won't have any money left to go out to dinner.

A bottle of whisky is an excellent soother of nerves—but don't let the removal men get their hands on it, or you'll have all your furniture chipped. A friend who had two particularly surly removal men made them a cup of tea and slipped two amphetamines into each mug. After that she had one of the jolliest moves imaginable.

How much to tip: about £1 a head—£2 if you're feeling affluent.

Do measure the height of the rooms before you go out and buy furniture in a sale. We had a tallboy standing in the street for weeks, because we couldn't get it through any of the doors.

If possible one of you should take a week off work (even if it is unpaid) to get things straight. Nothing is more demoralising than coming home late for the next month to face the chaos.

Try to get the kitchen and one other room habitable; then you can shut yourselves away from the débris when it becomes too much for you.

DO-IT-YOURSELF

One of the great myths of marriage—heavily fostered by television commercials of smiling young couples up ladders—is that home decorating is fun when you do it together.

It isn't. It's paralysingly boring and caused more rows in our marriage than anything else. Just remember that, like having a brace on your teeth as a child, it's worth it later on.

Invariably one partner is more hamfisted than the other, and the trouble starts when the more dexterous one becomes irritated and starts bossing poor Hamfisted about. Hamfisted gets more and more sulky until a row breaks out.

My husband is a great deal more adept than I am at decorating, but even so it was always a case of Wreck-it-Yourself. Our first attempts at wallpapering out-crazied the Crazy Gang. We lost our tempers, the measure and the scissors. I had bought enough paper

Our wrinkled, uneven labour

to do two rooms (wildly expensive at sixteen guineas a roll) but we had to scrap so much we only managed three quarters of one room. Finally when we stood back to admire our wrinkled uneven labours, we found we had papered the cat to the wall like the Canterville Ghost.

A FEW POINTS TO REMEMBER

Buy cheap wallpaper for your first attempts.
When you strip wallpaper and come to a layer of silver paper, leave it alone, or you'll find you've stripped off the damp course, and any paper subsequently put on the wall will turn green.

PAINTING

Do remember to put dust sheets down when you're painting or you'll get shortsighted aunts commenting on the attractive speckled border round the walls.

If you're doing the landing and the hall, don't as we did start painting the landing scarlet, and the hall indigo – it never entered our heads that the colours would have to meet somewhere, in this case halfway up the stairs. The result is horrible.

Go to a showroom where you can see the paint you choose in large quantities. That colour that looks so subtle on the shade card can spread to vast deserts of ghastliness once it gets up on the wall.

Don't mix paints unless you're an expert: they always come out sickly ice-cream shades.

Never get friends to help. Even your own pathetic attempts will be better than theirs. We let a girlfriend, who claimed she found painting therapeutic, loose on one of the spare rooms. When we looked in a quarter of an hour later, there were terracotta flames of paint licking a foot high over the virgin white ceiling I had painted the day before. None of our cries of "Steady on" or "I say" could halt her. The whole room had to be painted again.

Tell your wife before you paint a shelf or she'll bustle in five minutes later and replace everything you removed. You are bound to have a row about who didn't wash the brushes last time.

If you run out of paint, do remember the name and brand before you chuck the tin away. We had to buy five different shades of orange before we hit on the right one again.

Lots of praise is essential. Say well done even if it isn't; people get inordinately proud of the four square foot of wall they've just painted.

MISCELLANEOUS

Curtains were another disaster zone – in an attempt to make them not too short, I made them miles too long, so they trailed on the floor like a child dressing up in its mother's clothes. And of course there wasn't enough material left over for the pelmets.

Don't be fooled by do-it-yourself tiling kits: they're easy enough until you have to round a corner or meet a natural hazard like a light switch.

TRADITIONAL ROLE OF
HUSBAND AND WIFE

Traditionally the husband is the more practical and mechanically minded member of the partnership. But if he's the kind who hits the electricity main every time he knocks a nail in and puts up shelves at 10°, and his wife is the practical type who got a distinction for carpentry at school, she shouldn't hesitate to take over. As my husband remarked, here was one sphere in which he wouldn't have minded having his masculinity undermined.

Running the house

HOUSEKEEPING

A major problem for the newly married wife, particularly if she is holding down a nine-to-five job. Before she was married she blued her wages on clothes and took her washing home to Mummy every weekend. Now suddenly, she must be housekeeper, cook, hostess, laundress, seamstress, beguiling companion, glamour girl, assistant breadwinner and willing bedfellow all in one.

What she must remember when she gets home exhausted from the office to be faced with a mountain of washing up in the sink, the dinner to be cooked, the bed to be made, the flat to be cleaned, a pile of shirts to be ironed, and her husband in a playful mood, is that where marriage is concerned, CHEERFULNESS, SEXUAL ENTHUSIASM, AND GOOD COOKING are far nearer to Godliness than cleanliness about the house.

As long as the flat is kept tidy—men hate living in a muddle—meals are regular, and their wives are in good spirits, husbands won't notice a few cobwebs.

If you amuse a man in bed, he's not likely to bother about the mountain of dust underneath it.

RESENTMENT

If a wife feels resentful that she is slaving away, while her husband comes home and flops down in front of the television until dinner is ready, she must remember that it isn't all roses for him either.

He has given up his much prized bachelor status for marriage and he probably expects, like his father before him, to come home every night to a gleaming home, a happy wife, and a delicious dinner. Instead he finds a tearful, fractious shrew, and he forgets that his mother looked after his father so well because she didn't have to go out to work.

TOLERANCE

Tolerance is essential on both sides. If the wife is working the husband must be prepared to give her a hand. Equally, it's up to the wife to ask when she needs help, and not scurry round with set face like someone out of Foxe's Book of Martyrs. As men hate seeing their wives slaving, one of the solutions is for the wife to get her housework done when her husband isn't around.

That house-keeping whizz-kid Mrs. Beeton suggests getting up early, and I managed to persuade most of my employers to let me work from eight-thirty to four-thirty. Eight-thirty sounds horrendous, but once you're used to it, it's much the same as nine-thirty. You miss the rush-hour traffic both ways, you have a nice quiet hour in the office before anyone else gets in to ring your mother or make a shopping list (no-one knows whether you got in exactly at eight-thirty anyway) and you get home at least an hour before your husband so you have time to get the dinner on, tidy up and welcome him home.

Another solution is to encourage your husband to have at least one night out a week with the boys, then you have a few hours to catch up.

DAILY WOMEN

Or you can employ a daily woman. If you get a good one, hang on to her, she's worth her weight in bullion. Generally, alas, dailies start off marvellously and then after a few weeks the standard goes down and so does the level of the gin. My husband came home once and found ours asleep in our bed with the electric blanket and the wireless on.

Asleep in our bed

If I have a good daily, I find I spend far more time than before tidying up before she comes, and if I get a bad one, I spend hours tidying up after her, so my husband won't grumble about throwing money away and force me to sack her.

Dailies also have an irritating habit of not turning up the day your mother-in-law is coming to stay, or the time you're relying on them to tidy up before a large dinner party.

But to return to housework. Remember that the dust you flick away today will have drifted back into place tomorrow. Once when I was rabbitting on about the dirtiness of my house, a girlfriend, whose house is none too clean either, told me I was suffering from the bourgeois syndrome: namely, obsessive worrying over spit and polish. It worked like a charm. I didn't do any housework for at least a fortnight.

A FEW QUICK POINTERS
Have lots of cushions to hide things under when guests arrive, and plump them a great deal. The woman who

Huge arm muscles

has the tidiest house in London has huge arm muscles from plumping.

Closing untidy desks, straightening papers, putting books back vertically instead of horizontally and records back in their sleeves, picking things off the floor: all make a room look better quicker than dusting or hoovering.

Empty ashtrays, clear dirty glasses into the kitchen, open windows at night, or the place will smell like a bar parlour in the morning.

Get a decent hoover, or you'll be like a girlfriend who grumbled to her husband that she was quite exhausted from hoovering all day.

He looked around and said: "I wish you'd do some hoovering in our house instead then."

Don't hoover under his feet—it's grounds for divorce.

If your kitchen is a pigsty, don't have a glass door, or a hatch through which inquisitive guests can peer.

Don't use all the dusters for polishing silver or shoes, or you'll have to hare round before dinner parties dusting furniture with the front of your dress like I do.

LAUNDRY

If you can possibly afford it during the first six months, send your husband's shirts to the laundry; one of the things that nearly broke my back when I was first married was washing and ironing seven shirts a week. Do encourage your husband to buy dark shirts for the office, so he can wear them for at least two days.

If you wash by hand, don't, as I always do, put in far too much soap powder and spend the next two hours rinsing.

If you wash at the launderette, remember to put your money into the machine, or you'll come back forty minutes later to find your clothes still unwashed. Be careful not to put anything that runs into the machine. When we were first married I left in a red silk handkerchief. My husband's shirts came out streaked like the dawn, he wore cyclamen underpants for weeks and claimed he was the only member of his rugger fifteen with a rose pink jock strap.

If you have a spin dryer, remember to put a bowl under the waste pipe or you'll have the kitchen awash every time. Drying is a problem in a small flat; one of the most useful presents we had was a Hawkins Hi-Dri (which then cost about £9), which will dry all your washing in about six hours and can be folded away afterwards.

Husbands are not amused by singe marks. They can be removed with peroxide, and in an emergency use talcum powder. Always put ironing away when you've finished – either the cat is bound to come and sit on it, or it looks so badly ironed it gets mistaken for dirty laundry and washed again.

The ideal, of course, is to send everything to the laundry. Unfortunately our laundry is notorious for not getting things back on time (we've got very used to the rough male kiss of blankets) and for 'losing' things.

CLEANING

Try to keep all cleaning tickets in one place. We always lose them, and at this moment, half our wardrobe is sitting in various cleaners all over London, soon no doubt to be sold second-hand.

FOOD

I got the sack from my first job after I was married because I spent all morning on the telephone apologising to my husband for the row we'd had on the bus, and all afternoon reading recipe books.

Cooking well and cooking cheaply is a major problem for the young wife. Before she was married she probably invited her fiancé to dinner from time to time and blued half her wages on double cream and brandy to go with the fillet steak and the shellfish, so that he is under the illusion that she is a marvellous cook. Now she is married she will find cooking exciting meals every evening and not overtaxing her imagination and the family budget extremely difficult.

Don't, however, be seduced into buying things that are cheap if they repel you. I once bought a black pudding, because I was told it was inexpensive and nourishing. It lay like a long black slug in the fridge for three weeks, finally turned green, died and was committed to the dustbin.

Ring the changes: however much he raves over your fish pie, he won't want it twice a week for the next fifty years.

Buy in bulk if you and your husband have self control: we find bulk buying never does anything but increase our bulk. The joint that is bought on Saturday never graduates into cold meat and later shepherd's pie. It is always wolfed in one sitting. Once we made a big casserole to last a week. It took eight hours to cook, stank the whole block of flats out, and went bad the following day.

Buy in bulk

Leave long-cooking dishes to the weekend. Nothing irks a man more than having to wait until midnight to eat. Do take the stew off the gas before you start making love.

Never hide things—you won't remember where you put them. I hid some potted shrimps once and discovered them a month later after we'd had the floor boards up.

HUSBANDS

If you find a half bottle of wine in the kitchen, check before you drink it. Your wife may be saving it for cooking some exotic dish.

Don't be bossy in the kitchen. Nothing irritates a woman more than to be told to add some more paprika, or that your mother always made it with real mashed potato.

MONEY

Honesty about money is absolutely essential in marriage. If you are to avoid major rows, you must know how much money you've got in the bank, and how much each of you is spending.

In theory all bills should be kept together and paid at the end of each month. Weekly accounts should be kept and the financial situation should be reviewed every month.

In practice we never did any of these things. We both got married with overdrafts well into three figures—having lived at home I had no idea of the cost of living, and between us we were earning far less then £2,000 a year. We ricocheted from one financial crisis to another.

Economising is particularly hard when you're first married, for there are so many things to do to the house, and if the wife is determined to impress the husband with her cooking, it's cream and wine in everything.

We used to have absurd economy campaigns: drinking tea instead of coffee for breakfast, driving miles to find a garage which sold cheaper petrol, turning out the lights and creeping round in the dark to save electricity, smoking less (which meant we ate more), eating less (which meant we smoked more).

We did evolve a splendid bill-paying evasion technique.

We never paid a thing until we got a solicitor's letter; then we would send the creditor a cheque, unsigned, so they would spend another week returning it, whereupon it would be returned in successive weeks, with the date left off, the wrong year, or the numbers and letters differing.

Another ruse was to ring up when the final reminder turned up and say in aggrieved tones: "But I've already paid it", and they'll spend at least a month trying to trace it.

With electricity, gas and telephone, you can always write and query the amount, saying you've been away for the last month and you can't think why the bill is so high.

Perhaps the best method is to keep sending the bill back with 'Not known here' written across it.

I tried once to keep accounts and in the third week, when I was making great efforts to economise, I saw to my horror that the expenditure had doubled. I went sobbing to my husband, who pointed out quite kindly that I'd added the date in.

Try to pay the rates by the month—and why not investigate a household budget account with your bank manager? It considerably simplifies bill-paying.

Another minor money problem is that one always assumes that one's partner will have some money on him, and he never has, so you find you have to jump off buses because neither of you can pay the fare, or walk home five miles from parties in the middle of the night because you can't afford a taxi.

Remember that each partner is bound to think the other one extravagant, and that everyone always thinks he is broke, however rich he is. As one friend said the other day: "We're just as poor as when we were first married but on a grander scale."

SHOPPING

Shop early in the morning when there's more choice, and mid-week when things are cheaper.

Always make a list, or you'll have the absurd situation of trailing miles to Soho market in your lunch hour, then buying all the things you've forgotten on the way home – at Fortnums.

Don't let men go near the shops, they'll blue the week's housekeeping on salmon and rump steak and come home very smug because they've shopped so much more quickly than you would have done.

Take things out of your shopping bag and put them away at once, or you'll have frozen raspberries melting on to the drawing room carpet, and liver blood permanently on your cheque book.

Despite the maxim: "If you can get it on tick it's free, if you can pay by cheque it's almost free, but if you have to pay cash, it's bloody expensive," pay cash if you can. Our biggest shopping bill is always drink, because we can chalk it up at the off-licence round the corner.

Be tolerant of each other's extravagances. Everyone lapses from time to time. One of the nicest things about my husband is that he never grumbles about my buying a new dress unless he thinks it is ugly.

TIDINESS AND UNTIDINESS

If the husband is married to a real slut, who constantly keeps the house in a mess and serves up vile food, he has every right to complain. There's a happy medium between being a doormat and a bully. Rather than work yourself into a frenzy of resentment, first try to tease your wife out of her sloppiness, and if that doesn't work, risk a scene by telling her it just isn't good enough.

A firm hand

Women on the whole quite like a firm hand, and one of the saddest things a wife ever said to me was: "It was only on the day he left me that he told me for the first time that I was a lousy cook, I turned the place into a pigsty, I never ironed his shirts, and left mustard under the plates."

Men like a place they can relax in and if the wife is the tidy one, she shouldn't nag and fuss her husband the moment he gets home.

"I can't stand it any longer," said one newly married husband, "she's taken all my books and put them in drawers like my shirts."

"Among some of the best marriages," my tame psychiatrist told me, "are those in which, although the husband and wife started at relatively distant poles of neatness and sloppiness, they moved towards a common middle ground, through love, understanding and willingness to understand each other's needs."

If there's one thing I can't stand..."

CHANGING PEOPLE

You shouldn't go into marriage expecting to change people. Once a bumbler always a bumbler, once a rake always a rake (a gay eye isn't likely to be doused by marriage). Once a slut—although she may make heroic and semi-successful attempts to improve—always a slut. When we were first married, my husband used to dream of the day I stopped working in an office, like the Three Sisters yearning for Moscow: "The house will be tidy, we shall make love every morning, and at last I shall be given breakfast."

Well, I left the office, and chaos reigned very much as usual. It's a case of plus ça change, I'm afraid.

Your only hope is that by making people happier and more secure they may realise the potential inside them and develop into brilliant businessmen, marvellous lovers, superb cooks, or alas, even bores. And remember, the wife who nags her husband on to making a fortune won't see nearly so much of him. He'll be in the office from morn until night. She can't have it both ways.

117

DIFFERING TASTES

Certain things are bound to grate. He may have a passion for flying ducks and Peter Scott and she may go a bundle on coloured plastic bullrushes and a chiming doorbell.

The wife may also use certain expressions like "Pleased to meet you," which irritate her husband to death; or he may say "What a generous portion" every time she puts his food in front of him.

Now is the time to strike. If you say you can't stand something in the first flush of love, your partner probably won't mind and will do something about it. If, after ten years, you suddenly tell your husband it drives you mad every time he says: "Sit ye down" when guests arrive, he'll be deeply offended, and ask you why you didn't complain before.

IRRITATING HABITS

Everyone has some irritating habits – the only thing to do when your partner draws your attention to them is to swallow your pride and be grateful, because they may well have been irritating everyone else as well.

I have given up smoking and eating apples in bed, or cooking in my fur coat, and I try not to drench the butter dish with marmalade. My husband no longer spends a quarter of an hour each morning clearing the frog out of his throat, and if he still picks his nose, he does it behind a newspaper.

There are bound to be areas in your marriage where you are diametrically opposed. Compromise is the only answer. I'm cold blooded, my husband is hot blooded. I sleep with six blankets, he sleeps half out of the bed.

I like arriving late for parties so I can make an entrance, he likes arriving on the dot because he hates missing valuable drinking time. I can't count the number of quiet cigarettes we've had in the car, waiting for a decent time to arrive.

Don't worry too much that habits which irritate you now will get more and more on your nerves. My tame psychiatrist again told me: "Those quirks in one's marriage partner which annoy one in early days often become in later years the most lovable traits."

Rows

My husband and I quarrel very seldom except when we've had too much to drink. We both loathe rows and hate being shouted at. I was very worried when I first married because I read that quarrelling was one of the most common methods of relieving tensions in marriage, and was confronted with the awful possibility that our marriage had no proper tensions.

It is very hard to generalise about rows. Some of the happiest married people I know have the most blazing rows, and then make it up very quickly–like M.P.s who argue heatedly in the House all night, and then meet on terms of utter amicability in the bar five minutes later.

However much a row clears the air, one is bound during its course to say something vicious and hurtful, which may well be absorbed and brooded upon later. Try therefore to cut rowing down to the minimum. It will upset children when they come along, and if you row in public, it's boring and embarrassing for other people, and you won't get asked out any more.

We found the occasions when rows were most likely to break out were:

Friday night–both partners are tired at the end of the week.

Going away for weekends—one person is always ready and anxious to avoid the rush-hour, the other is frantically packing all the wrong things, so the first five miles of the journey will be punctuated with cries of 'Oh God' and U-turns against the ever-increasing traffic to collect something forgotten.

Weddings—the vicar's pep-talk in church on Christian behaviour in marriage always sets us off on the wrong foot. Then afterwards we'll be suffering from post-champagne gloom and wondering if we're as happy as the couple who've just got married.

Television—husband always wants to watch boxing, and the wife the play.

Desks—the tidy one will be irritated because the untidy one is always rifling the desk, and pinching all the stamps and envelopes.

Clothes—men not having a clean shirt, or clean underpants to wear in the morning.

Space in the bedroom—the wife will appropriate five and three quarters out of six of the drawers and three out of four of the coat hangers, and leave her clothes all over the only chair.

MINOR IRRITATIONS
ALL LIKELY TO CAUSE ROWS

The wife should avoid using her husband's razor on her legs and not washing it out, or cleaning the bath with his flannel, or using a chisel as a screwdriver, or pinching the husband's sweaters. There are also the eighteen odd socks in her husband's top drawer, the rings of lipstick on his best handkerchief, running out of toothpaste, loo paper, soap. Forgetting to turn out lights, fires, the oven. Forgetting to give her husband his letters or telephone messages.

MAKING UP

Never be too proud to apologize, but do it properly;

none of that "I've said I'm sorry, haven't I?", followed by a stream of abuse.

Don't worry about letting the sun go down on your wrath—it's no good worrying a row to its logical conclusion when you're both tired and then lying awake the rest of the night. Take a sleeping pill, get a good night's sleep and you'll probably have forgotten you ever had a row by morning.

Try not to harbour grudges, never send someone to Coventry.

A sense of humour is all-important for ending rows. My husband once in mid-row put both feet into one leg of his underpants and fell over. I went into peals of laughter and the row was at an end.

Once when I was threatening to leave him he looked reproachfully at the cat, and said: "But we can't let poor Tibbles be the victim of a broken home."

Poor Tibbles

A note on feminine problems

BLACK GLOOMS

Suffered particularly by wives in the first six months after marriage, they usually stem from exhaustion, feeling totally unable to cope, and reaction after the wedding. They are extremely tedious for the husband, but nothing really to worry about unless they linger on longer than a week. Nothing will be achieved by telling her sharply to snap out of it – patience, a lot of loving and encouragement are the only answer.

THE CURSE

Should be re-named the blessing. Every row two weeks before it arrives, and a week after it's finished, can be blamed on it.

ANNIVERSARIES

Husbands are notorious for forgetting birthdays and anniversaries. Don't expect a heart-shaped box of chocolates on Valentine's Day, but avoid a row over anniversaries by saying loudly about three days before: "What shall we do on my birthday/our anniversary on *Friday*, darling?"

Christmas

The row usually starts about September and continues through to February.

Wife: Where shall we go for Christmas, darling?

Husband: Anywhere you like, darling.

Wife: Well I thought we might spend a few days with Mummy.

Husband (appalled): With your mother! No drink,

and frost because we don't go to church
a day. If you think I'm staying with that c
Wife (interrupting with some asperity): Wl
have in mind?
Husband: Well I rather thought we mi
Scotland.
Wife: To stay with your parents! No central heating,
and those damned dogs–that's charming.
And the row follows its normal course.
Many people like to go to their families for Christmas
and they can't understand why their partners find it
such a strain. If you can't stand going to either set of
parents, get a large dog and say you can't leave it.

CHRISTMAS PRESENTS
These can be an awful bore, particularly if you come
from large families. We've evolved a system whereby
my husband buys all the men's presents, and I look
after the women and children.

Relations and friends

IN-LAWS
The ideal is to marry an orphan. However hard you
try, you'll probably have some trouble with your
in-laws. Mine have always been angelic to me but as
my mother-in-law pointed out to me in a moment of
candour, nobody is ever good enough to marry one's
children.
Be kind to your in-laws. Remember that many parents
are so involved with their children that it's an act of
infidelity almost tantamount to divorce when they
suddenly meet someone and marry them. For years a
mother has considered herself her daughter's or her

123

best friend, and suddenly she isn't. She sees them confiding in someone else, and as they draw further and further away from her, she becomes more and more unpleasant by trying to hang on to them.

Tact is essential. Be particularly nice to your husband/wife when in-laws are around, but don't neck and don't exclude them with private jokes. From the wife a bit of sucking up doesn't come amiss. Ask your mother-in-law's advice about cooking and washing, say your husband is always raving about her apple pie, how does she make it?

One thing that particularly upsets mothers-in-law is heavy eye make-up and long untidy hair, so if you want to take the business of getting on with her seriously, tie your hair back and soft pedal the make-up when you see her.

The husband's best tack is to flirt with his mother-in-law, even if she's an old boot. Few women can resist flattery.

Wives can flirt with their fathers-in-law, but don't overdo it, or you'll have your mother-in-law branding you a fast piece.

However much you dislike having your in-laws to stay, be philosophical about it: at least it will make you clean the place up. My mother-in-law once slept peacefully and unknowingly on a pillow-case full of wet washing. Don't give them too lush food or they'll think you're being extravagant. Herrings and cider will impress them far more than lobster and caviar. And hide those battalions of empties before they arrive.

My husband always takes his parents on a tour of the house, pointing out things that need repairing in anticipation of a fat cheque.

YOUR OWN PARENTS

However fond you are of your own parents, remember

that when a man marries 'he shall leave his father and mother and cleave unto his wife'.

Loyalty to your husband or wife must always come first. Don't chatter to your mother too long or too often on the telephone, it will irritate your husband and possibly make him jealous.

If you have a row with your husband or wife, and pack your bags, go to a discreet friend; never, never go home to your parents. You will say a lot of adverse things about your partner in the heat of the moment which you will forget afterwards, but your parents will remember them and it will be extremely difficult afterwards for your parents and partner to pick up the threads again.

FRIENDS

A friend married is a friend lost, goes the proverb, and certainly one of the sad facts of marriage is that it's almost impossible to keep up with friends one's other half doesn't like. You can relegate them to lunch dates and evenings when your partner is out, but invariably they get the message and sweep off in low-gear dudgeon.

Much of the first year of marriage is spent weeding out the sheep from the goats. Both parties should try not to be jealous of the other half's close friends. My husband certainly made short work of any friends he considered a) boring, b) unstable influences.

If you find your husband's friends a bore, establish a reputation for delicacy early on in the marriage, then when they lurch in drunkenly from the pub, you can plead exhaustion and disappear upstairs to read a book.

DROPPERS-IN

Ought to be abolished. People should telephone first

and see if you want to see them. No one will bother you the first month or so. They used to apologise to us for telephoning after seven o'clock, assuming we'd be in bed. After that they'll descend in droves, looking curiously for signs of strain in your faces, avid to see what kind of mess you've made of your flat.

One method of getting rid of them is to dispatch your husband to the bedroom, rip off all your clothes, ruffle your hair, and, clad only in a face towel, answer the door brandishing the Kama Sutra. The droppers-in will be so embarrassed that they'll apologise and make themselves scarce.

Entertaining notions

ENTERTAINING
Always check with your partner before you issue or accept an invitation, or you'll get ghastly instances of double dating.

Time and again recently, we've been making tracks for bed when the telephone goes, and an irate voice says, "Aren't you coming? We're all waiting to go in to dinner." Or we'll be just leaving the house to go out, when a rosy-cheeked couple arrive on the doorstep having driven fifty miles up from the country for dinner.

Keep a book by the telephone and write everything down.

DINNER PARTIES
Unless you're a Cordon Bleu cook, and totally unflappable, your first dinner parties are bound to be packed with incident. Overcooked meat, undercooked potato salad, soufflés that don't rise, guests that don't rise to the occasion.

If you're a beginner, cook as much as possible the day before. Cod's roe paté, liver paté, soup, casseroles and most puddings can all be made beforehand. Then all you have to do the following day is to make the toast and mix a salad dressing.

If possible get the table ready the night before as well.

Answering the door

Polishing glasses, ironing napkins, getting out plates and coffee cups all take longer than one would imagine. Get plenty of cheese, in case you haven't given people enough – I once fell up the stairs with the pudding and eight plates, and there was no cheese in the house.

Guests

Don't spend hours away from your guests. Nothing is less calculated to put them at their ease than a hostess who turns up red in the face after three-quarters of an hour, grabs a quick drink and disappears again.

One couple we went to dinner with both disappeared for an hour to peel grapes for the Sole Véronique, and the whole meal was served to an accompaniment of piped cream.

Be careful who you ask with whom: the day our vicar's wife came to dinner we invited a young man who regaled us for half the evening with details of the mating habits of the rhinoceros.

Don't become a slave to social ping-pong. Entertaining is wildly expensive and just because you had caviar and three kinds of wine at the Thrust-Pointers, don't feel you have to give them oysters and liqueurs when they come back to you.

If you're broke, warn people beforehand that it will only be spaghetti and Spanish Burgundy, then they can either refuse, bring a bottle or have a number of stiff drinks beforehand.

If you're worried about the food, drink for at least an hour and a half before you eat, and they'll be so tight they won't know what they're eating.

Equally, if you're supremely confident about your food, don't let them drink too much.

Don't play loud background music before dinner, it kills conversation. People can go to a concert if they want that sort of thing.

Never, never show slides.

IF THEY WON'T GO

The husband should make the first move by saying his wife is tired and sending her to bed. If that doesn't work, turn the central heating off.

If you don't like certain people, don't feel you have to ask them back. They'll get the message eventually. Life is too short to bother with people you really don't care for. You'll work up too much angst beforehand about having to see them, and too much spleen afterwards about how bored you were.

PARTIES

Make a list and stick to it. We always ask indiscriminately and have far too many people, both of us trying to smuggle in people the other one doesn't like.

Don't send out invitations. You can't ask everyone, and people get very sour if they see your invitations on other people's mantelpieces. Also, if you invite by telephone, you get a 'yes' or 'no' immediately, and people are notoriously bad at answering letters.

We once gave a drears' sherry party – with fatal consequences. All our undreary friends found out and were furious they hadn't been invited, and the drears discovered why they'd been asked, and were deeply offended. We were a bit short of friends that year.

One of the secrets of a good party is a few abrasive elements. Recently we went to an outstandingly successful 'bring-an-enemy' party.

Don't expect to enjoy your own parties, except in retrospect. All your guests will be too busy getting drunk and trying to make other guests to bother about you. Your function is to act as unpaid waiter and waitress: effecting introductions, rescuing people whose eyes are beginning to glaze whether they're bored or drunk, and watching people's drinks.

Do mix a cocktail that can be poured, or give them wine, otherwise you'll get in a terrible muddle remembering what everyone wants and start giving them whisky and tonic and gin and soda.

GOING TO PARTIES

Don't stand together all evening, it will upset your hostess. Check every twenty minutes to ensure your partner isn't standing alone, doesn't need rescuing from the local bore, isn't pinned to the wall by the local sex maniac.

If you want to dance cheek to cheek with the most attractive man/woman in the room, wait until your husband/wife is securely trapped on the sofa in another room.

If you catch your partner making a pass at someone, smile broadly as though it was an everyday occurrence, say, "Drink always takes him/her this way, he/she won't remember a thing about it next morning," and whisk him/her away smartly.

HOW TO LEAVE

There is bound to be a moment when you want to go home and your husband doesn't because he's having too good a time, or *vice versa*. One of you will just have to grin and bear it. Don't get into the habit of leaving independently, it looks bad, and is very expensive on taxis.

Overcome with lust

If you're both bored, intimate to your hostess that you've been overcome by lust and must leave. She will think her party has been a contributing factor and be delighted, particularly if you leave murmuring about the seductive atmosphere.

The office

OFFICE PARTIES

If husbands and wives aren't invited, be extremely careful. This is the moment when Mr. Chalcott in Accounts, who has been eyeing Mrs. Pointer in Personnel all the year, suddenly gets too much drink in him, makes a pass at her and the whole thing erupts into an affaire. Try not to get home too late, be careful to wipe lipstick off your cheek if you're a man, and replace your make-up carefully if you're a woman. The fact that Mr. Prideau in Packaging saw fit to pounce on you may be just Christmas high spirits, but it will worry your husband, who'll think it is normal procedure for the rest of the year.

If you go to your wife's or husband's office party, be as nice as possible to everyone. These people may seem draggy to you, but your husband's got to put up with them all the year round, and will get tremendous kudos if you're a success.

Be prepared for anything. My mother went to my father's office party once when he was in a very senior position. She was hotly pursued by a man from the boiler division in a Mickey Mouse mask, who kept tracking her down in the Paul Jones, tossing her up in the air, and crying, "I am your demon lover".

Hotly pursued

Be careful what you wear, look pretty but not outrageous. When I was newly married, I went to the Author's Ball at the Hilton in a party of my husband's grandest business colleagues. Very brown from the South of France, I wore a white strapless dress which was so tight, I didn't need a bra. The five-course dinner was too much for it. As I stood up to dance with one of the directors, it split, leaving me naked to the waist.

OFFICE RELATIONSHIPS

A husband spends far more of his waking life with his secretary, and the people he works with, than with his wife. It is the same for his wife if she goes out to work.

It is very easy to get crushes on people you work with. There's naturally proximity, there's the charm of the clandestine (we musn't let anyone in the office know), of working together for a common purpose, and finally, because men basically like to boss, and women to be bossed, there is the fatal charm of the boss/female employee relationship. For if you are used to obeying a man when he says "Take a letter", or "Make me a cup of coffee", you may find it difficult to say no when he says "Come to bed with me".

Bear in mind before you either pounce, or accept the pounce across the desk, that people aren't nearly so easy to live with as to work with, and you'd probably be bored to death with your boss or secretary if you had to spend twenty-four hours a day with them. It will also make things very awkward later if you go off them, while they still fancy you, or vice versa. You may be forced to leave a job you like.

Be very careful, too, not to let your husband or wife think that you are keen on someone in the office, or they will go through agonies of jealousy during the day, and raise hell every time you are kept late—even if you are working.

HAVING YOUR HUSBAND'S BOSS TO DINNER

The wife should pull out all the culinary stops and look as beautiful as possible.

But don't flirt with your husband's boss too much or you'll have him sending your husband abroad and coming round on his own!

Invite another amusing but socially reliable couple to

meet him. Then when you and your husband have to leave the room to dish up or pour drinks, he won't be left alone to examine the damp patches or the peeling wallpaper.

Give him plenty to drink but not too much, or he may become indiscreet about company politics, regret it next day and take against your husband.

General marital problems

COMMUNICATION

One of the beauties of marriage is that you always have someone to look after, and to look after you, to share your problems, and to tell – without boasting – when something good happens to you.

It is vital that couples should get into the habit of talking to each other and be interested in each other's activities, be it a game of cricket, an afternoon at the W.I., or a day at the office. If you are able to communicate on a daily level, you will find it much easier to discuss things when a major crisis blows up – like a husband losing his job, a sudden sexual impasse, or the television breaking down.

Nothing is more depressing than seeing married couples on holiday or dining together gazing drearily into space with nothing to say to one another – at best it's a shocking example to unmarried people.

I feel strongly that married women should try to set a good example to newlyweds or people about to get married. Nothing is more morale-lowering for the engaged girl than to be taken aside by a couple of bored and cynical married women and told how dreary marriage is, the only solution being infidelity or burying oneself in one's children. Rather in the same way women who have children often terrorise women who are pregnant for the first time with hair-raising stories of childbirth.

SEPARATION

In long separations from your husband or wife, there are all the problems of loneliness and fidelity. Even short separations–a week or a weekend–have their own difficulties.

When her husband goes away, a wife steels herself not to mind, and although she misses him, unconsciously she builds up other resources. She finds it is rather fun to read a novel until three o'clock in the morning, have time to get the house straight, watch what programmes *she* wants on television, not have to cook and wash, and be able to see all the people she is not allowed to see when her husband is at home.

Gradually as the time for her husband's return approaches, she gets more and more excited. She plans a special homecoming dinner, she buys a new dress and goes on a twenty-four hour diet so she will look beautiful. In her mind she has a marvellously idealised picture of his homecoming.

And then he arrives–hungover, grubby, exhausted, and if he's been to America or anywhere else where the time is different from ours, he'll be absolutely knackered. He won't want to do anything else but fall into bed and then only to sleep.

The wife is inevitably disappointed–this is no God returning, merely a husband, grumbling about the rings round the bath, bringing not passion and tenderness but a suitcase of dirty shirts.

Similarly, a husband returning to his wife after some time away will find that an ecstatic welcome is often followed by a good deal of sniping and bad temper. The wife will have stored up so much unconscious resentment at being deprived of his presence that she will take it out on him for a few days.

The only way to cope with après-separation situations is not to get panicky if your wife or husband acts strangely. It doesn't mean they've met someone else, they are just taking a bit of time to adjust to your presence again. In a small way, it's like starting one's marriage over again.

JEALOUSY

Once your life is centred round one person, it is very easy to become obsessively jealous. Try and keep your jealousy in check; it will only cause you suffering, and make things very difficult for your partner.

If you marry a very pretty girl, or a very attractive man, the fact has to be faced that people will still go on finding them attractive.

Give your wife a certain amount of rope, let her go out to lunch with other men, but start kicking up if it becomes a weekly occurrence with the same man. Never let her go out for drinks with a man in the evening unless it's business or an old friend, and draw the line at breakfast. If you are married to the sort of man who's always humiliating you by running after women at parties, you'll have to grin and bear it. He's probably just testing his sex appeal, like gorillas beat their chests. Before I was married, a girl friend and I used to divide men into open gazers and secret doers. You've probably got an open gazer, so thank your lucky stars you're not married to a secret doer.

If you have an ex-wife or an ex-lover, destroy all evidence before you get married again. Nothing is more distressing for a second wife than coming upon wedding photographs of you and your first wife looking idyllically happy.

However much you may want to reminisce about

your exes, keep it to a minimum, and if you ever have to meet any of your wife's or husband's exes, be as nice to them as possible. No one looks attractive when sulking.

BOREDOM

It was not my intention in this book to deal with marriage in relation to children, but I would like to say a brief word about Cabbage-itis, which is my name for the slough of despond a wife goes through when she has two or more very young children to look after. Invariably she's stuck in the country or a part of town where she has few friends, her husband is going out to work every day and meeting interesting people and she isn't, and she feels dull, inadequate and so bored she could scream.

The family budget won't stretch to any new clothes for her, so she feels it is impossible for her to look attractive. On the occasions when friends bring children over for the day, it seems to be all chaos and clamour. She spends days planning a trip to London, which invariably ends in disappointment: her clothes are all wrong, she's worn out after two hours shopping, the girl friend she meets at lunch can't talk about anything except people she doesn't know, and if she attempts to take the children she's exhausted before she's begun.

She and her husband can't afford to entertain much, but when they are asked out she finds she is so used to saying "No" and "Don't" to children all day, she is unable to contribute to the conversation.

If you are going through this stage – and I think it is one of the real danger zones of marriage – remember that it isn't going on for ever. The children will grow up, go to school, and you will have acres of free time to go back to work, catch up on hobbies, to make new friends. Whatever you do, don't let yourself go to seed. Looking pretty isn't new clothes, it's clean hair, a bit of make-up and a welcoming hug when your husband comes home in the evening.

Remember that your husband must always come first, even before the children. In your obsession with your domestic problems, don't forget that he probably isn't having a very easy time either: desperately pushed for money, harassed at work, buffeted back and forth in a train every day, coming home to a drab, fractious wife every night.

So don't catalogue your woes; when he arrives in the evening, concentrate on giving him a good time.

Try and go out at least once a week if it's only to the cinema. Try and read a newspaper, or at least listen to the headlines while you're doing the housework, so you won't feel too much out of touch.

If possible find something remunerative to do, even if it's only making paper flowers, typing, or framing pictures. Nothing is more depressing than poverty and if you can make the smallest contribution to the family budget it will be a boost to your morale.

Clothes

CLOTHES AND APPEARANCE

"The reason why so few marriages are happy," said misogynist Swift, "is because young ladies spend their time in making nets not cages."

No wife has any right to let herself go to seed after she's married. She bothered enough to look pretty while she was trying to hook her husband, so it's a poor compliment to him if she slackens up immediately he's hooked.

Remember that the world is full of pretty girls who are not averse to amorous dalliance, and if you want to keep your husband, you'll have to work hard to go on attracting him.

It's a case, of course, of shacking-up *à son goût*. Some men prefer their wives *au naturel*, others are like the husband who said to me: "The marvellous thing about old Sue is that she always looks as neat as a new pin. I've never seen her without make-up or slopping around in jeans."

Exotic clothes

Remember too that no man ever went off his wife because he saw a crowd of men round her. So always pull out the stops when you go to parties, or out in the evening, or pick your husband up from the office. It is important to him that other people think you're attractive.

And even if your husband does prefer you without make-up, put some on when you go to a party. You'll have to compete with all those pretty girls with their streaked hair and their three pairs of false eyelashes. Your husband won't be amused if he has to keep leaving the girl he's chatting up to look after you because you've been abandoned.

If a wife wants to jazz up her husband's wardrobe, her best method is to start giving him exotic clothes for his birthday. He'll never go and buy them of his own accord.

It is also up to husbands and wives to take an interest in each other's appearance. Tell your husband when he looks handsome, and even if you are the sort of man who can't tell a discarded false eyelash from a centipede, compliment your wife on her appearance when she buys a new dress or is tarted up to go out in the evening.

SEWING

Great row potential here.

Shirt buttons always fly off when the man is getting dressed in the morning, or last thing at night when you're both going to bed, so they never get sewn on. The wife will also plump for Terylene socks and say they are healthier and cheaper, and can be thrown away when they go into holes, to be told by her husband that his mother always darned his woollen ones.

If the wife really can't sew, she should just content herself with sewing on buttons, and send all major repairs to the cleaners, where they can be done for a few extra pence.

Holidays

Much of the chapter on honeymoons applies here. People are so grimly determined to enjoy every moment of their holidays that they feel dismayed and cheated if anything goes wrong.

You're probably both exhausted, particularly if you've only been married a short time, and have had all the strain of getting adjusted. You've been planning and looking forward to your holiday for ages, then you arrive at your destination and find you're so unused to doing nothing that it takes you at least a fortnight to unwind. Then it's time to go home again.

There is also the sex problem. Before you were married, holidays were always treated as safaris. The moment you boarded the train at Victoria, the sap started rising, the eye started roving on the lookout for a holiday playmate. After you're married, the hunting instinct dies very hard. As a friend of mine said: "Taking a married man to the South of France is rather like taking a foxhound to a meet on a lead and not letting him join in the chase."

I'm not a believer in retaliation but if your husband does get a crush on another girl on holiday—carrying her beachbag, always ready with a large towel when she comes up from the sea—your best answer rather than sulking is to take to the nearest gigolo. And if there isn't a gigolo to take, comfort yourself with the thought that holiday romances seldom last beyond the holiday.

Going on holiday with friends, of course, is one of the quickest ways of losing them. The most amiable people turn into absolute monsters when they've got too much spare time on their hands.

Everyone will either want to do different things (lying in the sun, sightseeing, skin diving, pony trekking, or

merely getting drunk) or else no one will admit what
they want to do, and go round looking martyred:
"What would you like to do today, my darling?"
"Anything *you* like, darling."
"Oh don't be awkward."
Particularly avoid going with people who are much
richer than you (you'll worry the whole time about
spending too much) or poorer than you (or you'll spend
your time grumbling about their meanness).
We went to France once in a party of twelve, all great
friends. It was a catastrophe. Meals were exactly like
being back at school: "Hands up for salade niçoise."
All the people who could speak French pulled rank on
the people who couldn't or didn't dare. All the wives
sulked because all the husbands had got crushes on the
one single girl, who was sulking because she couldn't
hook the one single man. Bad will was absolutely
rampant.
I am painting a gloomy picture of holidays, because I
think people often feel that if they've had a disastrous
holiday their marriage must be on the rocks. "If we
can't get on when we're on holiday," they say, "there
must be something radically wrong." Forget it.
Cheerful pessimism is the best approach to a holiday,
and console yourself that the most disastrous holidays
are always the funniest in retrospect.

HOW TO BEHAVE

On holiday there is invariably one who does the
planning – booking rooms, tickets etc. – and one who
resists being planned. If you're the resister, cut down
on the beefing, whether it's about the lack of soap,
coat-hangers, hot water, drawer space, bed space, or
amount of garlic in the food. Remember when in
Rome . . . and shut up about it.
Don't overdo the sun – holidays are meant for lots of

sex, and you won't feel like it if you wince every time you touch each other. And it's depressing to start peeling like a ticker-tape welcome as soon as you turn brown.

Travel is inclined to broaden the hips as well as the mind. Take a few loose tops and larger sized trousers. Take lots of books and sleeping pills. One often can't sleep in hot countries, and nothing is more depressing than to feel that all the good of your holiday is being wasted because of insomnia. Take entero-vioform, so you won't spend all night thundering to the lavatory like the Gadarene Swine.

Remember you won't be able to buy the Pill, or whatever you use, in a Catholic country. One couple were staying in a villa in Spain, and a particularly greedy guest came down one morning, found their contraceptive paste in the fridge, thought it was some exotic pâté and spread it on his toast for breakfast.

Go somewhere where there's something to do: a casino, the odd night club, boats to sail, etc.

Money should be shared and kept an eye on: nothing wrecks a holiday more than the constant fear that you may run out.

Husbands and wives should do their own packing to avoid endless recriminations about sponge bags, razors, and cameras left behind.

It's horrible coming home to a dirty untidy house. If you haven't got a daily, pay a chum a couple of quid to come in the day before you get home to give the house a going over.

Don't show slides. Don't bore everyone when you get back with stories of your holiday. My husband refuses to talk about it, and hangs a notice on his office door saying 'yes'.

BED

Bed/sex/intercourse/making love—call it what you like—is the cornerstone of marriage. If the sex side of a marriage is really good, you seldom hear of it breaking up. If you keep your partner happy in bed, he's unlikely to stray, and if he does he nearly always comes back.

Few people are born geniuses in bed—it is something you learn step by step, like a child learns to talk. The first essential is to be honest with one another. Don't pretend to be going into ecstasies of excitement if you are not, or your partner will automatically assume he is doing the right things to please you, and keep on doing them.

A wife—if she can possibly help it—shouldn't pretend to be having an orgasm if she is not. Although her husband will flop down satisfied beside her afterwards, she will unconsciously build up a resentment both against him for not seeing through the cheat, and against herself for cheating.

Of course it's not vital to have an orgasm every time you go to bed with a man, but the fact remains that it's much nicer if you do. It draws you together, it gives you a marvellous feeling, and it's the best sleeping pill in the world.

Another myth that must be shattered is that men are lustful beasts whose appetites must be slaked, and women have to endure it.

"Your father was very good to me and never bothered me much," Victorian mothers used to tell daughters who were about to get married. "Just shut your eyes and think of England."

Recent research, however, has discovered that women

can be just as highly sexed as men, need intercourse just as often, but in most instances are too inhibited to ask for it.

Nothing that two people do in their own home

A wife should therefore not be ashamed to take a wholehearted enjoyment in sex, ask for it often, and if her husband isn't forthcoming, to seduce him by making herself pretty, wearing sexy underwear, or simply by wandering round in the nude.

Don't be too fastidious. Nothing that two people who love each other do for their mutual enjoyment in the privacy of their own home can be wrong. If he's on a Lolita kick, pander to his whims and dress up in a gym tunic. If she's got a slave girl complex, tie her up and beat her before you make love to her.

Sex books are quite helpful but they always made us howl with laughter. They kept talking about the 'upright male member', which made us think of an incorruptible M.P.

Read as much pornography as you can get your hands on, not only to excite you, but to give you ideas. Marriage needs every novelty to keep it going. A man I know said his wife was absolutely sensational in bed for at least a month after she'd read *Fanny Hill*.

For beginners (see the chapter on the honeymoon) the thing to remember is to take things slowly. It may be six months or a year before you manage to establish a sexual rapport. It's only in books that the man goes on drilling all night, and suddenly the rock splits and the oil comes gushing out. Enthusiasm is nine-tenths of the battle, and perseverance. Kindness and gratitude are also essential. Tell your husband what doesn't work for you, but make pretty sure you tell him when it is good. If having the inside of your thighs stroked excites you, say so. Don't let him wait thirty years to find out.

On a Lolita kick

Once a year

HOW OFTEN

This is entirely up to you. Everyone lies about it if you ask them. I read in one book that the average man of thirty has sexual intercourse 2·8 times a week. When I told my husband, a rather smug gleam came into his eye, but he was curious to know what they did on the ·8 occasion.

On the other hand, one Indian sex manual says that during the first year of marriage couples should have intercourse three times a night for the first three months, twice a night for the next three months, and every night for the rest of the year. After which I suppose you die of exhaustion.

There's no rule. Sometimes you may get a jag and have each other a dozen times in a weekend, sometimes if you're both tired you may not feel like touching each other for a week or so.

HOW NOT TO LOOK IN BED

Curlers and great blobs of face cream are grounds for divorce—no woman need wear them. If you want curly hair, get a set of heated rollers. If you want a soft skin, put on face cream in the bath.

People should wash and clean their teeth before they go to bed, and have at least one bath a day. This may sound elementary, but it's amazing how many people don't, and, sweat fetishists apart, most people would rather make love to someone who smells and tastes good.

Have separate beds if you must, but never separate rooms. Once you get on to the separate rooms kick, it's so easy to shut yourself in every night and grow further and further away from your partner. If one of you snores, or is a bad sleeper and wants to read, have a bed made up in the spare room, so you can slip into it if you get really desperate about three o'clock in the morning.

Don't, however, get out of the habit of making love. Quite often if you've been snapping at each other you will find that once you sleep together everything will be all right again.

I met a girl the other day who boasted she only gives herself to her husband once a year on his birthday. A woman should be grateful that her husband wants her, and any woman who says 'I don't feel like it tonight' more than two days running, unless she's ill, pregnant or recovering from a baby, deserves to have an unfaithful husband.

Equally no man should deny his wife, if she obviously wants it. There's no excuse for the sort of career man—an American, as it happens—who will only sleep with his wife on Friday and Saturday, so he'll be fresh for work on the weekdays.

Another of the great myths about sex is that for the

first year you glut yourselves like someone working in a sweet shop, and after that the glamour wears off and you settle down to pastimes like bringing up children and gardening. In any good marriage, sex should get better and better as the years go by, even if you indulge in it marginally less often.

Affaires

Another great fallacy is that marriage stops you falling in love with people. It doesn't. One of the most happily married men I know says he was riddled with guilt because he developed a violent crush on a blonde staying in the same hotel while he was on honeymoon. If you were the sort of person who was always falling in love before marriage, you'll probably go on doing it afterwards. Don't panic—try to nip it in the bud early. Refuse to see the person concerned. It will tear your guts out for a few weeks, but you'll find you get over it, just as you got over the crushes you had before you were married.

If you fancy someone, and you know they fancy you, don't try and rely on mutual self-control. These things if allowed to develop invariably get out of hand and can escalate into nasty things like divorce. The most shortsighted remark ever made at the beginning of an affaire is: "You're happily married and I'm happily married, and if we have an affair, we're both adult enough not to let it get out of hand or anyone get hurt." This is rubbish. Someone always gets hurt, and it'll probably be you. And remember, once your husband or wife finds out you are having an affair with someone else it will cause them appalling unhappiness, and your marriage will never be the "glad confident morning" it was.

MUTUAL INFIDELITY

"Husbands are such a bore," said a friend of mine. "They always want to know who you're dating." Some couples manage to go their own way, making a pledge of mutual infidelity, but I cannot help feeling that one of the partners must be enjoying it more than the other.

If you must have affaires, be discreet. The cardinal sin is to be found out. And when it's all over and you're feeling a louse and you want to clear your conscience, don't indulge in tearful confessions to your husband and feel you've cleaned the slate. It will upset him quite unnecessarily.

DISCOVERY

If you do discover your husband is having an affaire with someone, and he doesn't know you know, play it cool. It may blow over. Remember, "the robb'd that smiles steals something from the thief."

If you find out, and your partner knows you know, the only solution is to raise hell, and insist that it stops immediately. Once you start condoning something like this, you're lost. Usually the jolt of your finding out and minding so much is enough to make him give up the other person, in which case welcome him home like the prodigal son, and *never never* reproach him again.

People often have affaires as a bid for more attention from their partners and purposely leave clues so that their partners will find out and be jolted into loving them more. So if you discover your husband is having an affaire with someone, have a look at your own behaviour before you blame him to see if it's you who's at fault.

A FEW PRACTICAL SUGGESTIONS

If your wife seems like a bolter, put her on the same passport, then you won't waste a fortune in air tickets getting her back.

If you suspect your partner is having an affair with a particular person, go into howls of immoderate laughter every time that person's name is mentioned. When they ask why you're laughing, laugh some more and say no one takes that idiot seriously. Nothing douses passion quicker than ridicule. I really fancied a man once, until someone pointed out he looked like Dracula.

DETECTION

There are a number of indications that your partner is having an affair with someone:

If your husband insists he's been lunching at the local with the boys, and comes home reeking of garlic, gets out a packet of matches with Dar Sor Stefano printed on it, and lights a king-size cigar when he normally smokes Players.

If he starts a pointless row at breakfast, so he can storm out of the house, and needn't come back until late.

If he suddenly starts working late consistently and comes home smelling of scent.

If he looks happy on Monday morning, and miserable on Friday night.

If he suddenly starts having a bath in the morning.

If the distance between the ends of his tie is different in the morning from the evening.

If he keeps making ridiculous excuses to buy more cigarettes during the weekend when there are plenty of packets in the house.

If there's a spate of wrong numbers, it may not be burglars . . .

If your wife after always dressing scruffily for the

office suddenly starts smartening herself up, shaving her legs, buying new underwear, and getting home late.

If she doesn't look dismayed when you say you're going to America for three weeks.

If she is home all day and the loo seat is up when you get home.

If she suddenly gets sexually revved up. Women are like machines, the more they're used the better they work.

If she starts suggesting you make love to her standing on your head, she may not have been reading the Kama Sutra.

If she starts leaving intellectual books by the bed, or tidying the house frantically in the morning . . .

If you have a man friend to stay, and he knows where to put things away when he's doing the drying up.

If you're both out at work and you come home and find the towels all tidy in the bathroom instead of scrumpled up as usual. Or if the cat isn't hungry . . .

If the cat isn't hungry

Coming unstuck

Everyone can make a mistake, and there's no point in a couple sticking together if they're miserable, even for the sake of the children, who would be much happier with one contented parent than two continually at war. Do try and distinguish, however, between a temporary bad patch, which all marriages go through, and a permanent rift. Divorce is very unpleasant and very expensive. A great deal of mud-slinging and bitterness will inevitably occur, and there's the nasty business of dividing friends and property.

So before you run off, whether it's with someone or not, make absolutely sure you want to go. Your partner may or may not take you back afterwards, and the longer you stay away the more difficult it will be to start again.

Another thing to remember is that it's very cold outside the matrimonial cage. One beautiful woman I know recently left her husband because she was bored and unhappy. She was back within six months.

When she was safely married, she had a wonderful time, having numerous affaires, being hotly pursued by hordes of men (for nothing is more attractive to a man than a bored, beautiful but safely married woman –all fun and no fear). Once she had left her husband the men who had been swarming round her weren't nearly so anxious to declare themselves, and she soon found it was back to single girl status with all the nagging worries of who was going to take her out the next night.

Sometimes an affaire can ventilate a marriage and make a couple appreciate each other more:

Another friend of mine became so infatuated with her lover that she left her husband. Next morning she and her lover went along to the lover's solicitor, who asked her if there was anything detrimental they could use against her husband in the divorce. Was he cruel? Did he neglect her? Did he have affaires with other women or beat her up?

She thought for a minute and then burst into tears, saying she couldn't think of anything wrong with him. She rushed out of the solicitor's office and went back to her husband, whom to her amazement she found absolutely devastated by her departure. They have been happily married ever since.

Breeding

"HAS TOM FERTILISED WENDY YET?" asked one of the small bridesmaids gazing at the bridal couple at a recent wedding.

Premature certainly, but it's amazing how many brides have to carry extra large bouquets these days.

An extra large bouquet

A girl I know who was married when she was eight months pregnant was given a year's subscription to the Nappy Service by her office as a wedding present. Although there will be a few raised eyebrows if a baby turns up before nine months have elapsed, particularly if it is a spanking ten pounder and cannot be fobbed off as premature, the fact remains that the moment you get back from your honeymoon, people will start expecting you to get pregnant.

Every time the wife looks tired, has a bilious attack or leaves a party early, people will start exchanging knowing looks.

If after two years nothing happens, the pressure will really be on. Hints are dropped about 'getting set in your ways', or 'too used to living on two incomes.' People will keep suggesting you move to the country and send you estate agents' lists of bijou residences with large gardens. Dire warnings will be given about the difficulty of having babies after the age of twenty-five.

After three years, you will be offered names of 'perfectly marvellous gynaecologists', and friends will say the wife is overtiring herself and ought to give up work. People will take her aside and say: "Don't you think Henry ought to see a doctor as well, darling?"

Parents-in-law will display angst about not having any grandchildren to talk about at bridge parties.

They should all realise that it's none of their business. Anyone who starts interfering on this subject deserves a flea in their ear.

If couples don't have children, it's either because they don't want to yet, or because they're trying and they can't. Not being able to have children, whether it's temporary or permanent, is extremely distressing. (There is something tragic and yet ridiculous about those abortive threshings night after night.) Outsiders should not contribute to this distress by asking stupid questions.

I couldn't have children and, after seven traumatic years of trailing from doctor to doctor, we finally in extreme trepidation adopted one. It has been an unqualified success. Within twenty-four hours of the child's arrival we were infatuated with him, and couldn't imagine life without him.

Everyone told us we were too set in our ways. You lead such a full life, they said. Too full? Too empty? Too full perhaps of empty things. Children are not nearly so much work as alarmist mothers crack them up to be, and they are more fun than one could believe possible.

One of the great revelations of my life was how immeasurably much better life was when one was married than unmarried. Another was how much better marriage is when one has children.

Conclusion

I am fully aware of the inadequacies of this book. Some aspects of marriage are covered very scantily and some not at all, and because I was writing about staying married, I have dwelt more on the pitfalls than on the very considerable joys of marriage.

"For everyone, and particularly for women and children," Cecil King wrote recently, "the essential basis for security and happiness is a loving home."

Marriage is not a battlefield, it is a partnership, and married people should be partners not rivals. And although it is important to be a reliable wage earner, a splendid cook, a good manager, and magnificent in bed, the most priceless gift one married person can give to another is a merry and a loving heart.

W. C. Sellar & R. J. Yeatman

1066 AND ALL THAT

A book that has itself become become part of our history.
The authors made the claim that "All the History you can
remember is in the Book"—and for most of us, they were
probably right. But it is their own unique interpretation
of events which has made the book a classic; the result is
an uproarious satire upon textbook history and our con-
fused recollections of it.

AND NOW ALL THIS

In *1066 and all That* Messrs Sellar and Yeatman set out
to provide a history book to end all history books—and
succeeded brilliantly. In this hilarious sequel they turn
their satirical pens to geography and general knowledge
with equal mastery.

HORSE NONSENSE

Messrs Sellar and Yeatman now turn their enquiring pens
to the subject of horses—and the people who ride, hunt
and punt on them. Non-riders will find *Horse Nonsense*
indispensable to their understanding of the topic: and
riders will discover a lot of astonishing things about the
Noble Animal which may have heretofore escaped them.

More top humour available in Magnum Books

These and other Magnum Books are available at your bookshop or newsagent. It case of difficulties orders may be sent to:

Magnum Books
Cash Sales Department
PO Box 11
Falmouth
Cornwall TR10 109EN

Please send cheque or postal order, no currency, for purchase price quoted and allow the following for postage and packing:

UK   19p for the first book plus 9p per copy for each additional book ordered, to a maximum of 73p.

BFPO & Eire   19p for the first book plus 9p per copy for the next 6 books, thereafter 3p per book.

Overseas customers   20p for the first book and 10p per copy for each additional book.

While every effort is made to keep prices low, it is sometimes necessary to increase prices at short notice. Magnum Books reserve the right to show new retail prices on covers which may differ from those previously advertised in the text or elsewhere.